# studysync®

## Reading & Writing Companion
### British Literature

## UNIT 3

## studysync®

**studysync.com**

Copyright © BookheadEd Learning, LLC
All Rights Reserved.

Send all inquiries to:
BookheadEd Learning, LLC
610 Daniel Young Drive
Sonoma, CA 95476

ISBN 978-1-97-016223-3

3 4 5 6 LMN 24 23 22

B

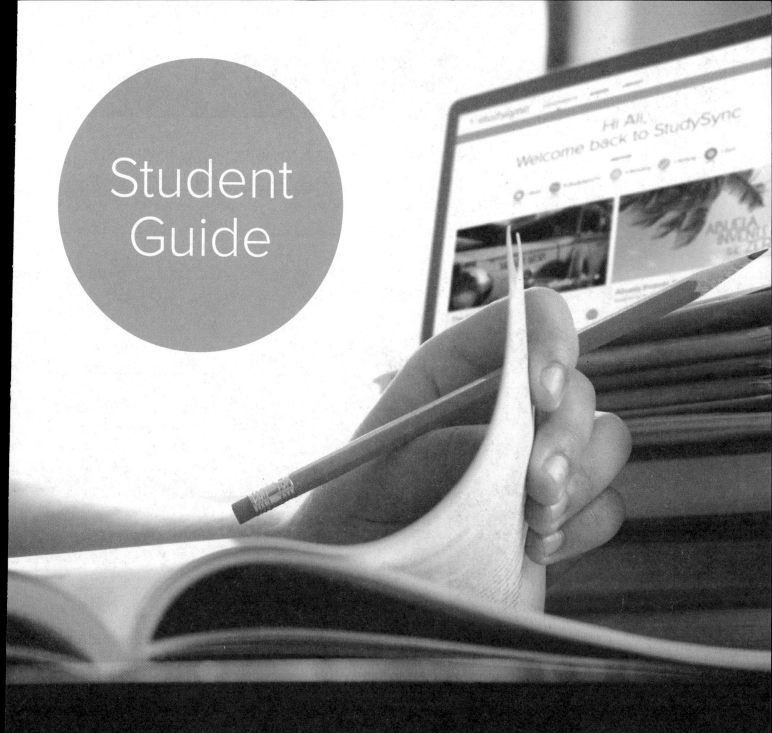

## Student Guide

# Getting Started

Welcome to the StudySync Reading & Writing Companion! In this book, you will find a collection of readings based on the literary focus of the unit you are studying. As you work through the readings, you will be asked to answer questions and perform a variety of tasks designed to help you closely analyze and understand each text selection. Read on for an explanation of each section of this book.

# Close Reading and Writing Routine

In each unit, you will read texts and text excerpts that are from or are in some way connected to a particular period of British literature. Each reading encourages a closer look through questions and a short writing assignment.

## 1 Introduction

An Introduction to each text provides historical context for your reading as well as information about the author. You will also learn about the genre of the text and the year in which it was written.

## 2 Notes

Many times, while working through the activities after each text, you will be asked to **annotate** or **make annotations** about what you are reading. This means that you should highlight or underline words in the text and use the "Notes" column to make comments or jot down any questions you have. You may also want to note any unfamiliar vocabulary words here.

You will also see sample student annotations to go along with the Skill lesson for that text.

  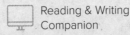

(3) # First Read

During your first reading of each selection, you should just try to get a general idea of the content and message of the reading. Don't worry if there are parts you don't understand or words that are unfamiliar to you. You'll have an opportunity later to dive deeper into the text.

(4) # Think Questions

These questions will ask you to start thinking critically about the text, asking specific questions about its purpose, and making connections to your prior knowledge and reading experiences. To answer these questions, you should go back to the text and draw upon specific evidence to support your responses. You will also begin to explore some of the more challenging vocabulary words in the selection.

(5) # Skills

Each Skill includes two parts: Checklist and Your Turn. In the Checklist, you will learn the process for analyzing the text. The model student annotations in the text provide examples of how you might make your own notes following the instructions in the Checklist. In the Your Turn, you will use those same instructions to practice the skill.

---

(3)  First Read

Read "The Pardoner's Prologue (from *The Canterbury Tales*)." After you read, complete the Think Questions below.

(4) **THINK QUESTIONS**

1. In stanza two, the Pardoner says, "Our liege-lord's seal on my patent perfect, / I show that first, my safety to protect, / And then no man's so old, no priest nor clerk, / As to disturb me in Christ's holy work." What can you infer about the Pardoner's attitude about the bulls, or official public decrees, that he carries? What purpose do they serve for him? Cite evidence from the text to support your explanation.

2. What are the two relics, or religious objects imbued with miraculous powers, that the Pardoner discusses? What are the specific alleged powers of these seemingly banal objects, according to the Pardoner? Cite evidence from the text to support your answer.

3. Citing the Pardoner's own words, what do you think he is most concerned about? How deeply is he invested in the salvation of his congregants?

4. The Latin word *pater* means "father." With this information in mind and using context clues from the text, write your best definition of the word **patriarch** here.

5. What is the meaning of the word **avarice** as it is used in the text? Write your best definition here, along with a brief explanation of how you arrived at its meaning.

---

(5)  Skill: Point of View

Use the Checklist to analyze Point of View in "The Pardoner's Prologue (from *The Canterbury Tales*)." Refer to the sample student annotations about Point of View in the text.

**••• CHECKLIST FOR POINT OF VIEW**

To grasp a character's point of view in which what is directly stated is different from what is really meant, note the following:

✓ Literary techniques intended to provide humor or criticism. Examples of these include:

- Sarcasm, or the use of language that says one thing but means the opposite
- Irony, or a contrast between what one expects to happen and what happens
- Understatement, or an instance where a character deliberately makes a situation seem less important or serious than it is
- Satire, or the use of humor, irony, exaggeration, or ridicule to expose and criticize people's foolishness or vices

✓ Possible critiques an author might be making about contemporary society through theme or characters' actions and words

✓ An unreliable narrator or character whose point of view cannot be trusted

To analyze a case in which grasping a point of view requires distinguishing what is directly stated in a text from what is really meant, consider the following questions:

✓ When do you notice that the reader's point of view differs from that of the character or speaker in this text?

✓ How does a character's or narrator's point of view contribute to a nonliteral understanding of

---

(5) **YOUR TURN**

1. The Pardoner uses figurative language when he states, "To spice therewith a bit my sermoning / And stir men to devotion, marvelling." Why does the Pardoner use this metaphor?

   ○ A. He uses the metaphor to explain how he makes his sermons more appetizing so he can better trick the churchgoers.
   ○ B. He uses the metaphor to explain the process of using potions and relics in the forgiveness of sin.
   ○ C. The metaphor serves to educate the churchgoers.
   ○ D. He uses the metaphor to persuade the churchgoers.

2. Which of the following phrases makes it clear that the Pardoner knows he is a liar?

   ○ A. "And, good sirs, it's a cure for jealousy;"
   ○ B. "Shall every sheep be healed that of this well / Drinks but one draught;"
   ○ C. "Then show I forth my hollow crystal-stones,"
   ○ D. "Relics are these, as they think, every one."

3. This question has two parts. First, answer Part A. Then, answer Part B.

   **Part A:** Which statement best reflects the relationship the Pardoner has with the churchgoers?

   ○ A. He respects them and seeks their advice on religious matters.
   ○ B. He tries to manipulate them and hide his true intentions.
   ○ C. He tries to help them but is concerned they won't accept it.
   ○ D. He believes they are intelligent but immoral.

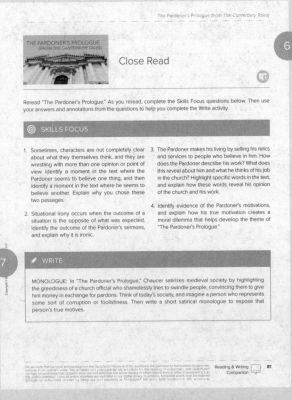

## Close Read & Skills Focus

After you have completed the First Read, you will be asked to go back and read the text more closely and critically. Before you begin your Close Read, you should read through the Skills Focus to get an idea of the concepts you will want to focus on during your second reading. You should work through the Skills Focus by making annotations, highlighting important concepts, and writing notes or questions in the "Notes" column. Depending on instructions from your teacher, you may need to respond online or use a separate piece of paper to start expanding on your thoughts and ideas.

## Write

Your study of each selection will end with a writing assignment. For this assignment, you should use your notes, annotations, personal ideas, and answers to both the Think and the Skills Focus questions. Be sure to read the prompt carefully and address each part of it in your writing.

# Extended Writing Project and Grammar

This is your opportunity to use genre characteristics and craft to compose meaningful, longer written works exploring the theme of each unit. You will draw information from your readings, research, and own life experiences to complete the assignment.

## 1 Writing Project

After you have read all of the unit text selections, you will move on to a writing project. Each project will guide you through the process of writing your essay. Student models will provide guidance and help you organize your thoughts. One unit ends with an **Extended Oral Project,** which will give you an opportunity to develop your oral language and communication skills.

## 2 Writing Process Steps

There are four steps in the writing process: Plan, Draft, Revise, and Edit and Publish. During each step, you will form and shape your writing project, and each lesson's peer review will give you the chance to receive feedback from your peers and teacher.

## 3 Writing Skills

Each Skill lesson focuses on a specific strategy or technique that you will use during your writing project. Each lesson presents a process for applying the skill to your own work and gives you the opportunity to practice it to improve your writing.

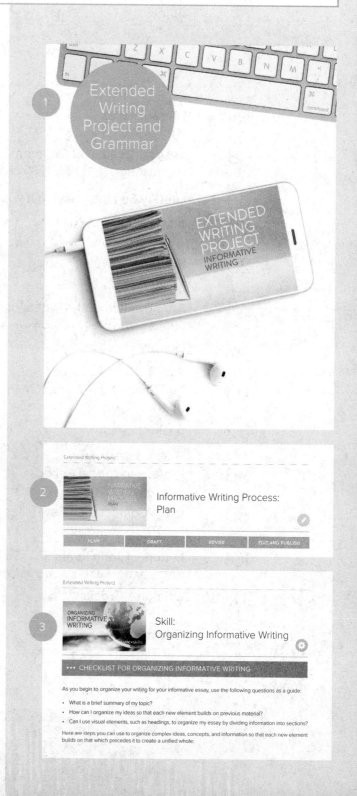

# Sculpting Reality

How do reason and emotion help us understand the world?

Literary Focus: THE ENLIGHTENMENT AND ROMANTICISM

## Texts

 PAIRED READINGS

# Extended Writing Project and Grammar

**Talk Back Text** are works from a later period that engage with the themes and tropes of the unit's literary focus. Demonstrating that literature is always in conversation, these texts provide dynamic new perspectives to complement the unit's more traditional chronology.

# Unit 3: Sculpting Reality
## How do reason and emotion help us understand the world?

### SAMUEL TAYLOR COLERIDGE

The youngest of fourteen children, Samuel Taylor Coleridge (1772–1834) was a leader of the British Romantic movement. Along with writing his own poetry, Coleridge was responsible for bringing some of the most influential writers of his time to prominence through his criticism—including poet William Wordsworth. Throughout his career, Coleridge merged politics with poetry, reacting to the consequential events of his day in verse.

### JOHN KEATS

When John Keats (1795–1821) abandoned his training as an apothecary and surgeon to become a poet, it was not at the encouragement of the literary community. In fact, Keats, who would go on to become among the most beloved English poets after his lifetime, was first received by critics as "unintelligible." Keats is best known for a series of odes, and he only wrote poetry seriously for about six years before succumbing to tuberculosis. His friend Percy Bysshe Shelley wrote the epic poem *Adonais* (1821) as an elegy for Keats in the days after his death.

### D. H. LAWRENCE

Prolific artist D. H. Lawrence (1885–1930) defies categorization. His vast output included poems, novels, short stories, plays, essays, travel books, and paintings. In these works, Lawrence turned a critical eye towards the industrial world that was rising up around him. His biting explorations of the dehumanizing effects of modern society led to censorship and exile during his life. Upon his death, however, novelist E. M. Forster dubbed Lawrence "the greatest imaginative novelist of our generation."

### JOHN LOCKE

Among the most influential philosophers and political theorists of the seventeenth century, John Locke (1632–1704) penned theories that inspired both the European Enlightenment and the United States Constitution. A proponent of limited government and religious tolerance, Locke argued that in order to understand the world around us, we must first understand ourselves. A graduate of the University of Oxford, Locke was one of the early members of the illustrious Royal Society, which counted contemporaries such as Sir Isaac Newton as members.

### MARY SHELLEY

The daughter of feminist author Mary Wollstonecraft and wife of poet Percy Bysshe Shelley, Mary Shelley (1797–1851) is best remembered for one novel that has captivated the imagination of generations of readers. Shelley conceived of the story in response to a challenge from Lord Byron, with whom she and her husband were spending the summer. In a moment of sleepless terror late one night, Shelley was visited by the vision of a doctor standing above a reanimated corpse. The next day, she sat down to write her first novel, *Frankenstein*.

## PERCY BYSSHE SHELLEY

English poet Percy Bysshe Shelley (1792–1822) was a literary icon of the Romantic era, which emphasized the importance of the imagination. He received an upper-class education and traveled throughout Europe as a young man. In addition to writing poetry and plays, Shelley also wrote political pamphlets, some of which he distributed with hot air balloons. He was married to Mary Shelley, the author of the novel *Frankenstein* (1818). Just before his thirtieth birthday, the poet drowned off the coast of Italy while sailing.

## JONATHAN SWIFT

Considered the greatest prose satirist in English literature, Anglo-Irish writer Jonathan Swift (1667–1745) is best known for his deadpan, ironic style. In *Gulliver's Travels*—widely regarded as his masterpiece—Swift employed his caustic wit as he critiqued human nature and the society of his time. By Swift's own account, he wrote *Gulliver's Travels* in order "to vex the world rather than divert it." Vexed or not, the public embraced Swift's work, and it has become the most widely held work of Irish literature in libraries around the world.

## MARY WOLLSTONECRAFT

Feminist writer and intellectual Mary Wollstonecraft (1759–1797) was born to a volatile home and set out to earn her own living at the age of twenty-one. Along with her sister, Eliza, and best friend, Fanny, Wollstonecraft founded a school in northern London. In 1792, Wollstonecraft published her essay *A Vindication of the Rights of Woman*, in which she argued that women should have access to the same educational opportunities as men—a truly revolutionary idea at the time.

## WILLIAM WORDSWORTH

William Wordsworth (1770–1850) published *Lyrical Ballads* with Samuel Taylor Coleridge in 1798, introducing Romanticism to English poetry with poems like Wordsworth's "Lines Composed a Few Miles above Tintern Abbey" and Coleridge's "The Rime of the Ancient Mariner." Wordsworth's love for the natural world was nurtured in his youth, when he lived in a house along the River Derwent in Northern England. The exploration of human connection to nature imbued his writings throughout his lifetime.

# The Enlightenment

## Introduction

This introduction provides readers with the historical and cultural context of the period of Enlightenment literature. The scientific progress that marked the sixteenth and seventeenth centuries paved the way for the Enlightenment, which is generally defined as the age of philosophy that figured most prominently in Europe during the 18th century. It was a time of scientific and social progress along with philosophical ideals that fostered the foundations of the United States of America.

# "Truth is not singular and does not come from a higher power."

*A Reading of Voltaire's Tragedy L'Orpheline de la Chine in the Salon of Madame Geoffrin;* painting of a French "salon" where intellectuals would gather to discuss literature and philosophy, by Anicet Charles Gabriel Lemonnier, ca. 1800

1   Just as the word *Renaissance* signifies the development of humanism in many different countries over several centuries, the term *Enlightenment* encompasses many thinkers and refers more to an idea than a specific time and place. Broadly defined, the Enlightenment is the age of **philosophy** that followed the scientific advancements of the Renaissance. The period was influential in Europe, especially in France, and in the American colonies. The Enlightenment period in Britain generally refers to the "long" eighteenth century, spanning the late-seventeenth to early-nineteenth century.

2   Known as the Age of Reason, the Enlightenment period was characterized by the belief that philosophy, which included the natural and social sciences, had the power to improve human life. In his essay "An Answer to the Question: What is Enlightenment?" (1784), German philosopher Immanuel Kant defines *enlightenment* as the movement of humans toward maturity. The mark of this maturity, according to Kant, is thinking for oneself. He believed that people could rely on their own intellect to figure out what to believe and how to act. Like Kant, other thinkers of the period also promoted new ways of thinking about truth, freedom, and equality, which ultimately ignited political movements.

NOTES

### The Roots of the British Enlightenment

3   Less than forty years after Queen Elizabeth I's death, England found itself facing bouts of civil war between royalists, who supported the monarchy of Charles II, and Parliamentarians. When the English Civil War drew to a close in 1660, Charles II was restored to the throne, and the government's rule by monarchy was left relatively unchanged. At the turn of the century, the monarchy would expand its power, as the kingdoms of England and Scotland officially joined to form a single kingdom, Great Britain, in 1707. In this political landscape, thinkers reappraised their ideas about how societies should be structured. The period originated theories of social contracts, which **posit** that individuals consent to be governed. This idea—that the right to rule is granted by individuals—contrasted sharply with the belief that monarchs possessed a divine right to rule.

4   English philosopher John Locke was particularly influential to later thinkers of the Age of Enlightenment. His *Two Treatises of Government* (1689) outlined ideas about personal freedom, **innate** rights, and separation of church and state. Locke was also concerned with ideas of truth and knowledge. Locke supported a view of gaining knowledge known as empiricism. Empiricism holds that we gain knowledge through direct observation and sensory experience, and it is considered a cornerstone of modern scientific experimentation. Debates over the ideas of empiricism flourished during the Enlightenment, with thinkers such as Irish clergyman George Berkeley (1685–1753) and Scottish philosopher David Hume (1711–1776) continuing the conversation.

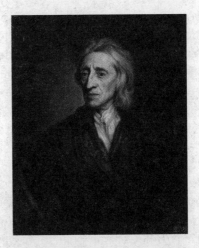

Portrait of John Locke by Godfrey Kneller, 1697

5   While several notable figures arose from the British Enlightenment, including Locke, Hume, Isaac Newton, Alexander Pope, and Jonathan Swift, on the whole, the Enlightenment had fewer tangible impacts on the British government than it did in other parts of the world. The heart of the

Enlightenment period, and its most significant effects, lay overseas in France and in the fledgling government of Britain's American colony, soon to become the United States.

### Philosophy with Revolutionary Consequences

6   The late eighteenth century was punctuated with social and political unrest, which influenced (and was influenced by) Enlightenment ideals. People wanted to think for themselves and have a say in how their governments functioned. This progress, some believed, meant that traditional structures, such as the monarchy, the privileged ruling class, and the political power of the Catholic Church, had to be removed. The clash between the new and the traditional violently erupted with the famous Storming of the Bastille on July 14, 1789, which marked the beginning of the French Revolution. Although the Enlightenment-era revolutions were historic moments and successful in many ways, they did not always result in a more equal and free society. The French revolutionaries, for example, wanted to replace the monarchy with a government by the people, but violence continued throughout the 1790s, leading eventually to Napoleon Bonaparte's crowning himself emperor in 1804.

*The Storming of the Bastille* by Jean-Pierre Houel, 1789

7   In the American colonies, the Founding Fathers were similarly inspired to seek more **egalitarian** modes of government. Enlightenment ideals in general, and the work of English philosopher John Locke in particular, became critical parts of the ideological underpinnings for revolution and the establishment of a new government. Locke had argued that "natural rights" meant no person, including the king, had the right to "harm another in his Life, Health, Liberty or Possessions." These words are echoed in the Declaration of Independence, which says "We hold these truths to be self-evident, that all men are created equal, that they are endowed by their Creator with certain unalienable Rights, that among these are Life, Liberty and the pursuit of Happiness." Like Locke, the colonists believed the power of any government

came from the people and, therefore, the people had the right to overthrow any government that violated people's natural rights.

### Enlightenment in the Arts

8   Much of the Enlightenment focused on the nature of experience, the influence of science, the role of reason, and the formation of new social and political systems, while the role of visual and literary arts was not at the forefront. The focus on order did, however, still influence the visual arts, which emphasized symmetry and simplicity and viewed art as an intellectual pursuit more so than an emotional one. Many Enlightenment thinkers discussed theories of aesthetics, or the nature of beauty. The age of philosophy was also the age of criticism. Philosophers developed specific criteria that could be used to determine whether an object should be considered beautiful. Much of the art during this time period was Neoclassical. Writers, musicians, painters, sculptors, and architects found inspiration in the classical beauty of ancient Greece and the Roman Empire.

9   **Major Concepts**

- **The Pursuit of Truth**—Most Enlightenment philosophy centers on the idea of "truth" and the work of humans to understand it. This is influenced by scientific progress and the development of the scientific method. Truth is not singular and does not come from a higher power. It is an abstract concept, but it is worthy of study. Through careful observation, experimentation, and logic, humans can better understand truth, and this understanding can improve the human **condition.** The study of truth involves many different fields of knowledge—the natural world, the human body, human behavior, the role of governments, and the formation of just societies.

- **The Pursuit of Liberty**—The revolutions that took place during the eighteenth century sought to create free and equal societies that respected the will of the people. Although these ideals did not always work out in reality, the pursuit of liberty was a powerful force for progress and change. Themes of liberty and freedom are explored throughout the literary and informational texts of the time period. Artists and philosophers looked back to ancient Greece and Rome to find inspiration in these great civilizations. They respected the wisdom and reason of ancient philosophers as they looked toward the future, imagining new knowledge, technology, and structures that could continue to improve human life.

10  **Style and Form**

- **Rhetoric and Rhetorical Devices**—Rhetoric is the art of speaking and writing persuasively. Classical rhetoric uses three types of appeal: *logos,* an appeal to logic; *pathos,* an appeal to the emotions of the audience;

and *ethos,* an appeal based on the author's expertise. Authors and speakers often use rhetorical devices, such as similes, metaphors, alliterations, allusions, and repetitions, to help them persuade their audience. These techniques help readers and listeners better understand and relate to what an author is trying to say.

- **Satire**—Satire is a way of criticizing something—a person, an idea, a tradition, a political structure, a social custom—by making it ridiculous. Creating a satire often requires verbal irony, that is, stating one thing and meaning the opposite. The Enlightenment's focus on improving human life often involved noticing what needed to be changed. Satirists highlighted these necessary changes by presenting the ridiculousness of things as they were. Writer Jonathan Swift defined a specific deadpan style of satire. His fictional *Gulliver's Travels* is an account of the strange customs Gulliver encounters; however, they reflect British society as Swift observed it. For instance, Swift mocks the cronyism of Britain's political parties when he shows the Lilliputians making court appointments based solely on style of a person's shoes.

Gulliver walks through a Lilliputian city in this 1904 illustration by Stephen Baghot de la Bere (1877–1927).

11 The ideas of the Enlightenment changed the course of history and continue to influence societies and governments around the world today. The Enlightenment's focus on the scientific method and the pursuit of knowledge ushered in an age of rapid industrialization, the effects of which, from the incredible developments in technology and medicine to the challenges posed by pollution, are important aspects of the twenty-first century.

12　The artistic impact of the Enlightenment is arguably overshadowed by that of the Renaissance before it and the Romantic period that would follow. It's influences can, nonetheless, still be seen today. Governmental sponsorship of scientific pursuits and the emphasis on learning led to significant changes that are still felt today. From questioning the divine right of kings, to embracing modes of inquiry that still underlie the scientific method, the Enlightenment changed the way people related to the world around them. Likewise, Swiftian satire can still be seen in a wide variety of media. Movies, television, websites, online newspapers, blogs, and tweets all satirize politicians, celebrities, mainstream news outlets, and countless other aspects of modern life. Just as in the age of philosophy, we continue to pursue truth and liberty, hoping to make human experience just a little better each day.

# Literary Focus

Read "Literary Focus: The Enlightenment." After you read, complete the Think Questions below.

 **THINK QUESTIONS**

1. What were the main goals of the Enlightenment? Cite evidence from the text to support your answer.

2. How did Enlightenment ideals affect the United States of America? Cite evidence from the text to support your answer.

3. How did the Enlightenment impact public speaking? Cite specific evidence from the text in your answer.

4. Use context clues to determine the meaning of the word **innate** as it is used in the text. Write your definition of *innate* here, along with those words from the text you used to determine its meaning. Then check a dictionary to confirm your understanding.

5. The Latin root *aequalis* means "equal." Keeping this in mind, what do you think the word **egalitarian** means? What are some other words with the same root, and what do they mean? Write your best answer here.

Please note that excerpts and passages in the StudySync® library and this workbook are intended as touchstones to generate interest in an author's work. The excerpts and passages do not substitute for the reading of entire texts, and StudySync® strongly recommends that students seek out and purchase the whole literary or informational work in order to experience it as the author intended. Links to online resellers are available in our digital library. In addition, complete works may be ordered through an authorized reseller by filling out and returning to StudySync® the order form enclosed in this workbook.

Reading & Writing Companion 7

Second
Treatise of
Government

INFORMATIONAL TEXT
John Locke
1689

## Introduction

British political philosopher John Locke (1632–1704) was one of the most influential thinkers of the Age of Enlightenment, a cultural movement that began in the late 17th century and emphasized individualism and reason over tradition. Originally published anonymously, *Two Treatises of Government* became one of Locke's most well-known works. In the first treatise, Locke argues against absolute power for the monarchy. The second treatise provides Locke's outline for a better form of government—one that protects the natural rights of citizens and derives its power from the consent of the governed. This excerpt is taken from the second treatise, which deeply influenced Thomas Jefferson, the principal author of the Declaration of Independence.

# "... being all equal and independent, no one ought to harm another in his life, health, liberty, or possessions ..."

NOTES

**from Chapter II: Of the State of Nature**

1  Sect. 4. To understand political power right, and derive it from its original, we must consider, what state all men are naturally in, and that is, a state of perfect freedom to order their actions, and dispose of their possessions and persons, as they think fit, within the bounds of the law of nature, without asking leave, or depending upon the will of any other man.

2  A state also of equality, wherein all the power and jurisdiction is reciprocal, no one having more than another; there being nothing more evident, than that creatures of the same species and rank, **promiscuously** born to all the same advantages of nature, and the use of the same faculties, should also be equal one amongst another without subordination or **subjection,** unless the lord and master of them all should, by any manifest declaration of his will, set one above another, and confer on him, by an evident and clear appointment, an undoubted right to dominion and sovereignty.

. . .

3  Sect. 6. But though this be a state of liberty, yet it is not a state of licence: though man in that state have an uncontroulable liberty to dispose of his person or possessions, yet he has not liberty to destroy himself, or so much as any creature in his possession, but where some nobler use than its bare preservation calls for it. The state of nature has a law of nature to govern it, which obliges every one: and reason, which is that law, teaches all mankind, who will but consult it, that being all equal and independent, no one ought to harm another in his life, health, liberty, or possessions . . .

. . .

**from Chapter VIII: Of the Beginning of Political Societies**

4  Sect. 95. Men being, as has been said, by nature, all free, equal, and independent, no one can be put out of this estate, and subjected to the political power of another, without his own consent. The only way whereby

any one **divests** himself of his natural liberty, and puts on the bonds of civil society, is by agreeing with other men to join and unite into a community for their comfortable, safe, and peaceable living one amongst another, in a secure enjoyment of their properties, and a greater security against any, that are not of it. This any number of men may do, because it injures not the freedom of the rest; they are left as they were in the liberty of the state of nature. When any number of men have so consented to make one community or government, they are thereby presently incorporated, and make one body politic, wherein the majority have a right to act and conclude the rest.

5    Sect. 96. For when any number of men have, by the consent of every individual, made a community, they have thereby made that community one body, with a power to act as one body, which is only by the will and determination of the majority: for that which acts any community, being only the consent of the individuals of it, and it being necessary to that which is one body to move one way; it is necessary the body should move that way whither the greater force carries it, which is the consent of the majority: or else it is impossible it should act or continue one body, one community, which the consent of every individual that united into it, agreed that it should; and so every one is bound by that consent to be concluded by the majority. And therefore we see, that in assemblies, impowered to act by positive laws, where no number is set by that positive law which impowers them, the act of the majority passes for the act of the whole, and of course determines, as having, by the law of nature and reason, the power of the whole.

from Chapter IX: Of the Ends of Political Society and Government

6    Sect. 123. If man in the state of nature be so free, as has been said; if he be absolute lord of his own person and possessions, equal to the greatest, and subject to no body, why will he part with his freedom? Why will he give up this empire, and subject himself to the dominion and controul of any other power? To which it is obvious to answer, that though in the state of nature he hath such a right, yet the enjoyment of it is very uncertain, and constantly exposed to the invasion of others: for all being kings as much as he, every man his equal, and the greater part no strict observers of equity and justice, the enjoyment of the property he has in this state is very unsafe, very unsecure. This makes him willing to quit a condition, which, however free, is full of fears and continual dangers: and it is not without reason, that he seeks out, and is willing to join in society with others, who are already united, or have a mind to unite, for the **mutual** preservation of their lives, liberties and estates, which I call by the general name, property.

7    Sect. 124. The great and chief end, therefore, of men's uniting into commonwealths, and putting themselves under government, is the preservation of their property. To which in the state of nature there are many things wanting.

from Chapter XIX: Of the Dissolution of Government

8   Sect. 232. Whosoever uses force without right, as every one does in society, who does it without law, puts himself into a state of war with those against whom he so uses it; and in that state all former ties are cancelled, all other rights cease, and every one has a right to defend himself, and to resist the aggressor. This is so evident, that Barclay[1] himself, that great assertor of the power and sacredness of kings, is forced to confess, That it is lawful for the people, in some cases, to resist their king; and that too in a chapter, wherein he pretends to shew, that the divine law shuts up the people from all manner of rebellion. Whereby it is evident, even by his own doctrine, that, since they may in some cases resist, all resisting of princes is not rebellion. His words are these . . .

9   Sect. 233. But if any one should ask, must the people then always lay themselves open to the cruelty and rage of tyranny? Must they see their cities pillaged, and laid in ashes, their wives and children exposed to the tyrant's lust and fury, and themselves and families reduced by their king to ruin, and all the miseries of want and oppression, and yet sit still? Must men alone be debarred the common privilege of opposing force with force, which nature allows so freely to all other creatures for their preservation from injury? I answer: Self-defence is a part of the law of nature; nor can it be denied the community, even against the king himself: but to revenge themselves upon him, must by no means be allowed them; it being not agreeable to that law. Wherefore if the king shall shew an hatred, not only to some particular persons, but sets himself against the body of the commonwealth, whereof he is the head, and shall, with intolerable ill usage, cruelly tyrannize over the whole, or a considerable part of the people, in this case the people have a right to resist and defend themselves from injury: but it must be with this caution, that they only defend themselves, but do not attack their prince: they may repair the damages received, but must not for any provocation exceed the bounds of due reverence and respect. They may repulse the present attempt, but must not revenge past violences: for it is natural for us to defend life and limb, but that an inferior should punish a superior, is against nature. The mischief which is designed them, the people may prevent before it be done; but when it is done, they must not revenge it on the king, though author of the villany. This therefore is the privilege of the people in general, above what any private person hath; that particular men are allowed by our adversaries themselves (Buchanan[2] only excepted)

---

1. **Barclay** sixteenth-century researcher of law William Barclay (1546–1608) wrote a well-known treatise on what he believed was the divine right of kings
2. **Buchanan** Scottish historian and scholar George Buchanan (1506–1582) wrote a revolutionary doctrine asserting that kings receive their power from the citizenry and that tyranny must be met with popular resistance

to have no other remedy but patience; but the body of the people may with respect resist intolerable tyranny; for when it is but moderate, they ought to endure it.

10   Sect. 234. Thus far that great **advocate** of monarchical power allows of resistance.

## ✏ WRITE

INFORMATIVE: Explain John Locke's perspective in *Second Treatise of Government*. What are his key ideas? What arguments does Locke use to convince the reader? Cite evidence from the text to support your explanation.

# Saying It with Satire

## Introduction

This text offers an exploration of satire in its many forms. Satire has been a literary genre for many centuries—dating back to the ancient Greeks. From Grecian critiques to the modern *Saturday Night Live* television series, satire is a common artistic avenue for bringing attention to social issues in a comical way. With exaggeration, irony, and even ridicule, writers and artists suggest sly messages in their humorous stories.

# "Satire has been an influential art form as long as there have been social problems to criticize."

1 "On Wednesdays, we wear pink." So begins the transformation of Cady Heron, the main character of cult classic *Mean Girls,* from a math-loving homeschooler to a lipstick and gossip-obsessed "Queen Bee." Although it was first released in 2004, *Mean Girls* remains a popular and oddly insightful movie. Through a **mode** called satire, its over-the-top depictions of popularity and revenge act as a criticism of high school social politics and bullying.

2 Satire has been an influential art form as long as there have been social problems to criticize. As a means to question the people, ideas, and institutions in power, satire has filled an important and universal need. As such, the satire of a period can provide a window into the culture of the time, showing both the ideas that dominate the period and the voices that would challenge those ideas. Plato[1] even recommended a satirical play by Aristophanes[2] as a way to understand the Athenian constitution, and modern academics continue to analyze the play as a window into the way certain thinkers (sophists[3]) were viewed at the time.

The theatre of Herod Atticus in Athens, Greece. In ancient Greece and Rome, plays were a source of public entertainment and political critique.

1. **Plato** along with his mentor Socrates and his pupil Aristotle, Plato was one of the foundational philosophers of ancient Greece and founded the Academy, believed to be the Western world's very first institute of higher learning
2. **Aristophanes** a comic playwright of ancient Greece
3. **sophists** professional teachers of philosophy and rhetoric in ancient Greece

Copyright © BookheadEd Learning, LLC

3 Although there is a wide variety of work that has earned the label of satire, generally it is a form of artful, humorous social criticism with the goal of bringing attention to a subject or changing society in some way. While satire is largely directed at politics and political figures, it has also been used to critique religion and social dynamics and norms. To accomplish this, satire often recasts characteristics of the object of criticism in ways that are ridiculous or amusing, like holding up a funhouse mirror. Because satire uses irony or sarcasm to make its point, it can sometimes be difficult to determine whether or not the writer is being serious. The telltale hallmarks of satire are visible in the writer's use of irony, exaggeration, ridiculous situations, and illogical reasoning. The reader of satire must consider the subtext and the social context of what is being said. Often the writer imitates the point of view they mean to critique, and so actually holds the opposite view from what is written.

Satirical political cartoons use exaggeration and symbolism to critique political situations. This cartoon comments on reconciliation between England and France by showing English Minister William Pitt and French Emperor Napoleon Bonaparte dividing the world between themselves.

4 Because satire aims to expose problems and social **contradictions,** it is necessarily subversive in its authorial purpose. Unlike other forms of humor that imitate a source without critique, such as **parody** and teasing, satire aims to take power away from and direct judgement toward its subject. It points out that a person, situation, or practice does not measure up to a standard set by the satirist. Satire may be the tool of choice when an author feels that an issue has not been given enough attention, has become a part of the status quo, or would not respond to straightforward criticism. Satirists know that by making the subject of criticism seem laughable, they will reach their audience in a more effective way than they could otherwise.

5 For example, an article published on the satirical news website *The Onion* titled "'How Bad For The Environment Can Throwing Away One Plastic Bottle Be?' 30 Million People Wonder" satirizes the tendency to rationalize and think individualistically about negative habits that collectively have a large impact.

Please note that excerpts and passages in the StudySync® library and this workbook are intended as touchstones to generate interest in an author's work. The excerpts and passages do not substitute for the reading of entire texts, and StudySync® strongly recommends that students seek out and purchase the whole literary or informational work in order to experience it as the author intended. Links to online resellers are available in our digital library. In addition, complete works may be ordered through an authorized reseller by filling out and returning to StudySync® the order form enclosed in this workbook.

Reading & Writing Companion 15

The headline works as satire because of the contradiction between the individual thought, quoted in the first sentence, and the immediate acknowledgement that it is not just "one plastic bottle" but millions. An added layer of exaggeration flags the headline as satire, not a serious statement, when it suggests that thirty million people are all thinking the exact same thing. The unusually self-aware phrasing may be unrealistic, but the critique comes from maintaining a ring of truth. The result may make an audience chuckle and realize that they, too, may be prone to this kind of thinking.

### History of Satire

6   Satire is not a new development and has been a popular style of writing used to challenge power since ancient times. The ancient Romans first used the word *satire* to refer to a specific style of poetry and later began to apply it to a wider group of **critical** work. Two Romans were particularly influential in establishing major forms of satire. One was the poet Horace, whose satire criticized social vices and faux-pas in order to teach and educate through gentle humor. Juvenal, on the other hand, wrote satire that was a harsh criticism of social and political evils. He was less concerned with humor, and his form of satire attacked not only social structures but also individuals.

7   Satirical works can be found across many periods of literary history and have been a staple of British literature since the medieval period. Geoffrey Chaucer's *The Canterbury* Tales was a popular satirical work. Chaucer satirized religious figures, such as a nun and a pardoner, in order to critique corruption within social institutions like the Church. The Renaissance period in continental Europe featured political satire, while in Elizabethan England, writers rejected the genre as rude, and instead used more straightforward means of criticizing the legal system and life at court.

Modern musical production of *Candide* showing Candide, Voltaire, and dancers. Performed in Berlin, November 2018.

8    Satire blossomed in the Enlightenment. During this period of social and political examination, satire leaned toward the more political Juvenalian style. The French satirist Voltaire penned a satirical novella, *Candide,* which lampooned the overly optimistic mood of the period and criticized religious persecution. In Britain, a group of satirists, including Alexander Pope and Jonathan Swift, called themselves the Scriblerus Club. They wrote under the pseudonym Martinus Scriblerus, a character who was a terrible writer and who overused academic jargon. Swift's experience in the Scriblerus Club is apparent in one of his most well-known works, *Gulliver's Travels,* when Gulliver meets with members of a faraway academy. Gulliver praises the "great communicativeness" of one professor, who offers the chance to observe him "employed in a project for improving speculative knowledge, by practical and mechanical operations," while a professor in the school of language shares an inane proposal "to shorten discourse, by cutting polysyllables into one, and leaving out verbs and participles." After the publication of *Gulliver's Travels* in the eighteenth century, writers strove to imitate the satirical novel's style and artistic intent. Swift is also well-known for his work "A Modest Proposal," which is an early example of journalistic satire.

9    Satire has enjoyed other moments of particular popularity, especially at times when social institutions have undergone rapid change. One such moment occurred at the end of the 1950s, as the British Empire effectively came to an end. As the United Kingdom reevaluated its identity and place in the world, it also saw a rise of anti-establishment comedy. A well-reviewed revue by a group of students from Oxford and Cambridge led to a "satire boom" in the United Kingdom, even leading to a popular television program, *That Was the Week That Was,* on the BBC.

10   More recently, satirical news programs have been a popular form of social and political criticism. *Saturday Night Live* fans will be familiar with that program's "Weekend Update," which has been parodying and satirizing real news stories since 1975. Other examples include Comedy Central's *The Daily Show* and *The Colbert Report.* These shows are not just an American phenomenon: countries such as Canada, Australia, Germany, Egypt, India, Italy, and Hungary have all produced satirical news TV programs or websites.

## Curbing Satirical Speech

11   Satire has long been an influential genre of writing, bringing attention to social issues and sparking conversations and action in response. Historically, however, it has also been met with censorship. Juvenal, for example, was exiled from Rome in the first century for his work. Voltaire's *Candide* was originally published in secret and was immediately banned because of its religious content. Swift also published his works anonymously. In the United States, the Alien and Sedition Acts of 1798 were passed as a reaction to

Please note that excerpts and passages in the StudySync® library and this workbook are intended as touchstones to generate interest in an author's work. The excerpts and passages do not substitute for the reading of entire texts, and StudySync® strongly recommends that students seek out and purchase the whole literary or informational work in order to experience it as the author intended. Links to online resellers are available in our digital library. In addition, complete works may be ordered through an authorized reseller by filling out and returning to StudySync® the order form enclosed in this workbook.

Reading & Writing
Companion

17

satirical criticism. The Sedition Act made it illegal to **defame** the elected president and Congress, effectively protecting the Federalist party, which was then in power, from criticism. Although the Sedition Act was quickly repealed, satirical speech in the twenty-first century is not entirely free from tension. Worldwide, satirical speech can still result in social pressure or threats and acts of physical violence. Despite this history of backlash, satire is still a popular and powerful tool for writers and artists to question the status quo and ask their audience to do the same.

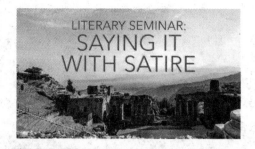

# Literary Seminar

Read "Literary Seminar: Saying It with Satire." After you read, complete the Think Questions below.

## ☁ THINK QUESTIONS

1. In the text, the author claims that "satire is not a new development." What else does the author say to support this statement? Use evidence from the text to support your answer.

2. How does the author separate satire from other forms of humor, such as parody and teasing? Support your answer by using evidence from the text.

3. Why can satire sometimes be difficult to understand? Reference specific details in the text in your response.

4. The noun **contradictions** is derived, in part, from the Latin verb *contradicere,* which means "to speak against." Using this information along with the word's context, write your best definition of *contradictions* here, along with a brief explanation of your reasoning.

5. Read the following dictionary entry:

**critical**

crit•i•cal /ˈkrid-ək-(ə)l/

*adjective*

1. containing or expressing negative views or condemnation
2. highly important to the existence or functioning of something
3. in a serious or potentially disastrous state

Use context to determine which of these definitions most closely matches the use of **critical** in the text. Write the correct definition of *critical* here, and explain how you determined its meaning.

# A Modest Proposal

ARGUMENTATIVE TEXT
Jonathan Swift
1729

## Introduction

Though engaged in English politics throughout most of his adult life, author Jonathan Swift (1667–1745)—a member of a distinguished London literary circle that included Alexander Pope, John Gay, and Joseph Addison—was, at heart, an Irishman. Born and educated in Dublin, he held a keen interest in the economic hardships facing the Irish working class, publishing his most famous satirical essay, "A Modest Proposal," anonymously in 1729. In it, Swift mocks heartless attitudes toward the plight of Ireland's poor by satirically suggesting that poor families sell their infants for food.

# "...a young healthy child well nursed, is, at a year old, a most delicious nourishing and wholesome food..."

NOTES

1   It is a melancholy object to those, who walk through this great town, or travel in the country, when they see the streets, the roads and cabbin-doors crowded with beggars of the female sex, followed by three, four, or six children, all in rags, and importuning every passenger for an alms. These mothers instead of being able to work for their honest livelihood, are forced to employ all their time in stroling to beg sustenance for their helpless infants who, as they grow up, either turn thieves for want of work, or leave their dear native country, to fight for the Pretender in Spain,[1] or sell themselves to the Barbadoes.

2   I think it is agreed by all parties, that this prodigious number of children in the arms, or on the backs, or at the heels of their mothers, and frequently of their fathers, is in the present deplorable state of the kingdom, a very great additional **grievance;** and therefore whoever could find out a fair, cheap and easy method of making these children sound and useful members of the common-wealth, would deserve so well of the publick, as to have his statue set up for a preserver of the nation.

3   But my intention is very far from being confined to provide only for the children of professed beggars: it is of a much greater extent, and shall take in the whole number of infants at a certain age, who are born of parents in effect as little able to support them, as those who demand our charity in the streets.

4   As to my own part, having turned my thoughts for many years, upon this important subject, and maturely weighed the several schemes of our projectors, I have always found them grossly mistaken in their computation. It is true, a child just dropt from its dam, may be supported by her milk, for a solar year, with little other nourishment: at most not above the value of two shillings, which the mother may certainly get, or the value in scraps, by her lawful occupation of begging; and it is exactly at one year old that I propose to provide for them in such a manner, as, instead of being a charge upon their parents, or the

---

1. **Pretender in Spain** a nickname for James Francis Edward Stuart, the son of the recently deposed King James II, who claimed to be the true heir of the British throne and was a figure of hope and revolution for the Irish people

parish, or wanting food and raiment[2] for the rest of their lives, they shall, on the contrary, contribute to the feeding, and partly to the cloathing of many thousands.

5　There is likewise another great advantage in my scheme, that it will prevent those voluntary abortions, and that horrid practice of women murdering their bastard children, alas! too frequent among us, sacrificing the poor innocent babes, I doubt, more to avoid the expence than the shame, which would move tears and pity in the most savage and inhuman breast.

6　The number of souls in this kingdom being usually reckoned one million and a half, of these I calculate there may be about two hundred thousand couple whose wives are breeders; from which number I subtract thirty thousand couple, who are able to maintain their own children, (although I apprehend there cannot be so many, under the present distresses of the kingdom) but this being granted, there will remain an hundred and seventy thousand breeders. I again subtract fifty thousand, for those women who miscarry, or whose children die by accident or disease within the year. There only remain an hundred and twenty thousand children of poor parents annually born. The question therefore is, How this number shall be reared, and provided for? which, as I have already said, under the present situation of affairs, is utterly impossible by all the methods hitherto proposed. For we can neither employ them in handicraft or agriculture; we neither build houses, (I mean in the country) nor **cultivate** land: they can very seldom pick up a livelihood by stealing till they arrive at six years old; except where they are of towardly parts, although I confess they learn the rudiments much earlier; during which time they can however be properly looked upon only as probationers:[3] As I have been informed by a principal gentleman in the county of Cavan, who protested to me, that he never knew above one or two instances under the age of six, even in a part of the kingdom so renowned for the quickest proficiency in that art.

7　I am assured by our merchants, that a boy or a girl before twelve years old, is no saleable commodity, and even when they come to this age, they will not yield above three pounds, or three pounds and half a crown at most, on the exchange; which cannot turn to account either to the parents or kingdom, the charge of nutriments and rags having been at least four times that value.

8　I shall now therefore humbly propose my own thoughts, which I hope will not be liable to the least objection.

9　I have been assured by a very knowing American of my acquaintance in London, that a young healthy child well nursed, is, at a year old, a most delicious

---

2. **raiment** articles of clothing
3. **probationers** new hires at a job who are currently undergoing a trial period before full employment

nourishing and wholesome food, whether stewed, roasted, baked, or boiled; and I make no doubt that it will equally serve in a fricasie, or a ragoust.

10  I do therefore humbly offer it to publick consideration, that of the hundred and twenty thousand children, already computed, twenty thousand may be reserved for breed, whereof only one fourth part to be males; which is more than we allow to sheep, black cattle, or swine, and my reason is, that these children are seldom the fruits of marriage, a circumstance not much regarded by our savages, therefore, one male will be sufficient to serve four females. That the remaining hundred thousand may, at a year old, be offered in sale to the persons of quality and fortune, through the kingdom, always advising the mother to let them suck plentifully in the last month, so as to render them plump, and fat for a good table. A child will make two dishes at an entertainment for friends, and when the family dines alone, the fore or hind quarter will make a reasonable dish, and seasoned with a little pepper or salt, will be very good boiled on the fourth day, especially in winter.

11  I have reckoned upon a medium, that a child just born will weigh 12 pounds, and in a solar year, if tolerably nursed, encreaseth to 28 pounds.

12  I grant this food will be somewhat dear, and therefore very proper for landlords, who, as they have already devoured most of the parents, seem to have the best title to the children.

13  Infant's flesh will be in season throughout the year, but more plentiful in March, and a little before and after; for we are told by a grave author, an **eminent** French physician, that fish being a prolifick dyet,[4] there are more children born in Roman Catholick countries about nine months after Lent, the markets will be more glutted than usual, because the number of Popish[5] infants, is at least three to one in this kingdom, and therefore it will have one other collateral advantage, by lessening the number of Papists[6] among us.

14  I have already computed the charge of nursing a beggar's child (in which list I reckon all cottagers, labourers, and four-fifths of the farmers) to be about two shillings per annum, rags included; and I believe no gentleman would repine to give ten shillings for the carcass of a good fat child, which, as I have said, will make four dishes of excellent nutritive meat, when he hath only some particular friend, or his own family to dine with him. Thus the squire will learn to be a good landlord, and grow popular among his tenants, the mother will have eight shillings neat profit, and be fit for work till she produces another child.

---

4. **prolifick dyet**  archaic spelling for *prolific diet*, a reference to the belief that eating fish could boost fertility
5. **Popish**  Roman Catholic
6. **Papists**  a negative term used to describe Roman Catholics

15   Those who are more thrifty (as I must confess the times require) may flea the carcass; the skin of which, artificially dressed, will make admirable gloves for ladies, and summer boots for fine gentlemen.

16   As to our City of Dublin, shambles may be appointed for this purpose, in the most convenient parts of it, and butchers we may be assured will not be wanting; although I rather recommend buying the children alive, and dressing them hot from the knife, as we do roasting pigs.

17   A very worthy person, a true lover of his country, and whose virtues I highly esteem, was lately pleased, in discoursing on this matter, to offer a **refinement** upon my scheme. He said, that many gentlemen of this kingdom, having of late destroyed their deer, he conceived that the want of venison might be well supply'd by the bodies of young lads and maidens, not exceeding fourteen years of age, nor under twelve; so great a number of both sexes in every country being now ready to starve for want of work and service: And these to be disposed of by their parents if alive, or otherwise by their nearest relations. But with due deference to so excellent a friend, and so deserving a patriot, I cannot be altogether in his sentiments; for as to the males, my American acquaintance assured me from frequent experience, that their flesh was generally tough and lean, like that of our school-boys, by continual exercise, and their taste disagreeable, and to fatten them would not answer the charge. Then as to the females, it would, I think, with humble submission, be a loss to the publick, because they soon would become breeders themselves: And besides, it is not improbable that some **scrupulous** people might be apt to censure such a practice, (although indeed very unjustly) as a little bordering upon cruelty, which, I confess, hath always been with me the strongest objection against any project, how well soever intended.

18   But in order to justify my friend, he confessed, that this expedient was put into his head by the famous Salmanaazor, a native of the island Formosa, who came from thence to London, above twenty years ago, and in conversation told my friend, that in his country, when any young person happened to be put to death, the executioner sold the carcass to persons of quality, as a prime dainty; and that, in his time, the body of a plump girl of fifteen, who was crucified for an attempt to poison the Emperor, was sold to his imperial majesty's prime minister of state, and other great mandarins of the court in joints from the gibbet, at four hundred crowns. Neither indeed can I deny, that if the same use were made of several plump young girls in this town, who without one single groat to their fortunes, cannot stir abroad without a chair, and appear at a play-house and assemblies in foreign fineries which they never will pay for; the kingdom would not be the worse.

19   Some persons of a desponding spirit are in great concern about that vast number of poor people, who are aged, diseased, or maimed; and I have

Copyright © BookheadEd Learning, LLC

been desired to employ my thoughts what course may be taken, to ease the nation of so grievous an incumbrance. But I am not in the least pain upon that matter, because it is very well known, that they are every day dying, and rotting, by cold and famine, and filth, and vermin, as fast as can be reasonably expected. And as to the young labourers, they are now in almost as hopeful a condition. They cannot get work, and consequently pine away from want of nourishment, to a degree, that if at any time they are accidentally hired to common labour, they have not strength to perform it, and thus the country and themselves are happily delivered from the evils to come.

20　I have too long digressed, and therefore shall return to my subject. I think the advantages by the proposal which I have made are obvious and many, as well as of the highest importance.

21　For first, as I have already observed, it would greatly lessen the number of Papists, with whom we are yearly over-run, being the principal breeders of the nation, as well as our most dangerous enemies, and who stay at home on purpose with a design to deliver the kingdom to the Pretender, hoping to take their advantage by the absence of so many good Protestants, who have chosen rather to leave their country, than stay at home and pay tithes against their conscience to an episcopal curate.

22　Secondly, The poorer tenants will have something valuable of their own, which by law may be made liable to a distress, and help to pay their landlord's rent, their corn and cattle being already seized, and money a thing unknown.

23　Thirdly, Whereas the maintainance of an hundred thousand children, from two years old, and upwards, cannot be computed at less than ten shillings a piece per annum, the nation's stock will be thereby encreased fifty thousand pounds per annum, besides the profit of a new dish, introduced to the tables of all gentlemen of fortune in the kingdom, who have any refinement in taste. And the money will circulate among our selves, the goods being entirely of our own growth and manufacture.

24　Fourthly, The constant breeders, besides the gain of eight shillings sterling per annum by the sale of their children, will be rid of the charge of maintaining them after the first year.

25　Fifthly, This food would likewise bring great custom to taverns, where the vintners will certainly be so **prudent** as to procure the best receipts for dressing it to perfection; and consequently have their houses frequented by all the fine gentlemen, who justly value themselves upon their knowledge in good eating; and a skilful cook, who understands how to oblige his guests, will contrive to make it as expensive as they please.

26  Sixthly, This would be a great inducement to marriage, which all wise nations have either encouraged by rewards, or enforced by laws and penalties. It would encrease the care and tenderness of mothers towards their children, when they were sure of a settlement for life to the poor babes, provided in some sort by the publick, to their annual profit instead of expence. We should soon see an honest emulation among the married women, which of them could bring the fattest child to the market. Men would become as fond of their wives, during the time of their pregnancy, as they are now of their mares in foal, their cows in calf, or sow when they are ready to farrow; nor offer to beat or kick them (as is too frequent a practice) for fear of a miscarriage.

27  Many other advantages might be enumerated. For instance, the addition of some thousand carcasses in our exportation of barrel'd beef: the propagation of swine's flesh, and improvement in the art of making good bacon, so much wanted among us by the great destruction of pigs, too frequent at our tables; which are no way comparable in taste or magnificence to a well grown, fat yearly child, which roasted whole will make a considerable figure at a Lord Mayor's feast, or any other publick entertainment. But this, and many others, I omit, being studious of brevity.

28  Supposing that one thousand families in this city, would be constant customers for infants flesh, besides others who might have it at merry meetings, particularly at weddings and christenings, I compute that Dublin would take off annually about twenty thousand carcasses; and the rest of the kingdom (where probably they will be sold somewhat cheaper) the remaining eighty thousand.

29  I can think of no one objection, that will possibly be raised against this proposal, unless it should be urged, that the number of people will be thereby much lessened in the kingdom. This I freely own, and 'twas indeed one principal design in offering it to the world. I desire the reader will observe, that I calculate my remedy for this one individual Kingdom of Ireland, and for no other that ever was, is, or, I think, ever can be upon Earth. Therefore let no man talk to me of other expedients: Of taxing our absentees at five shillings a pound: Of using neither cloaths, nor houshold furniture, except what is of our own growth and manufacture: Of utterly rejecting the materials and instruments that promote foreign luxury: Of curing the expensiveness of pride, vanity, idleness, and gaming in our women: Of introducing a vein of parsimony, prudence and temperance: Of learning to love our country, wherein we differ even from Laplanders,[7] and the inhabitants of Topinamboo:[8] Of quitting our animosities and factions, nor acting any longer like the Jews, who were murdering one another at the very moment their city was taken: Of

---

7. **Laplanders**  an English term for Finnish speaking people from a region in northern Europe called Lapland
8. **Topinamboo**  a region in Brazil populated with indigenous tribes

being a little cautious not to sell our country and consciences for nothing: Of teaching landlords to have at least one degree of mercy towards their tenants. Lastly, of putting a spirit of honesty, industry, and skill into our shop-keepers, who, if a resolution could now be taken to buy only our native goods, would immediately unite to cheat and exact upon us in the price, the measure, and the goodness, nor could ever yet be brought to make one fair proposal of just dealing, though often and earnestly invited to it.

30    Therefore I repeat, let no man talk to me of these and the like expedients, 'till he hath at least some glympse of hope, that there will ever be some hearty and sincere attempt to put them into practice.

31    But, as to my self, having been wearied out for many years with offering vain, idle, visionary thoughts, and at length utterly despairing of success, I fortunately fell upon this proposal, which, as it is wholly new, so it hath something solid and real, of no expence and little trouble, full in our own power, and whereby we can incur no danger in disobliging England. For this kind of commodity will not bear exportation, and flesh being of too tender a consistence, to admit a long continuance in salt, although perhaps I could name a country, which would be glad to eat up our whole nation without it.

32    After all, I am not so violently bent upon my own opinion, as to reject any offer, proposed by wise men, which shall be found equally innocent, cheap, easy, and effectual. But before something of that kind shall be advanced in contradiction to my scheme, and offering a better, I desire the author or authors will be pleased maturely to consider two points. First, As things now stand, how they will be able to find food and raiment for a hundred thousand useless mouths and backs. And secondly, There being a round million of creatures in humane figure throughout this kingdom, whose whole subsistence put into a common stock, would leave them in debt two million of pounds sterling, adding those who are beggars by profession, to the bulk of farmers, cottagers and labourers, with their wives and children, who are beggars in effect; I desire those politicians who dislike my overture, and may perhaps be so bold to attempt an answer, that they will first ask the parents of these mortals, whether they would not at this day think it a great happiness to have been sold for food at a year old, in the manner I prescribe, and thereby have avoided such a perpetual scene of misfortunes, as they have since gone through, by the oppression of landlords, the impossibility of paying rent without money or trade, the want of common sustenance, with neither house nor cloaths to cover them from the inclemencies of the weather, and the most inevitable prospect of intailing the like, or greater miseries, upon their breed for ever.

NOTES

33    I profess, in the sincerity of my heart, that I have not the least personal interest in endeavouring to promote this necessary work, having no other motive than the publick good of my country, by advancing our trade, providing for infants, relieving the poor, and giving some pleasure to the rich. I have no children, by which I can propose to get a single penny; the youngest being nine years old, and my wife past child-bearing.

## ✏ WRITE

INFORMATIVE: In "A Modest Proposal," Swift uses satire to critique prevailing attitudes toward the poor. Using Swift's essay as inspiration, choose a current social problem, and write your own "modest proposal," posing a satirical solution and critique. Let Swift's style and tone serve as a model to guide your own argument.

# Gulliver's Travels

FICTION
Jonathan Swift
1726

## Introduction

*Gulliver's Travels* is a masterpiece of satire, critiquing the popular 18th-century Enlightenment notion that advances in human society are the result of reason and logic alone. Through Lemuel Gulliver's voyages to fantastical lands, author Jonathan Swift (1667–1745) suggests the importance of religion and compassion in the guidance of human affairs. In this excerpt from Part I, Swift offers a thinly veiled mockery of 18th-century English politics: Lilliput, an island of miniature people engaged in ridiculous conflicts, is likely to symbolize the Kingdom of England, with the two major political parties of England—the Tories and Whigs—represented by Lilliput's High Heels and Low Heels. Rival island Blefuscu symbolizes the Kingdom of France.

# "It began upon the following occasion."

Copyright © Bookheaded Learning, LLC

**NOTES**

**Skill:**
Word Meaning

*What is a vessel? It is the object of a prepositional phrase, so I know it's a noun. I see words like* boat, swam, *and* tide. *These are context clues that a vessel relates to the sea, but I'm still not sure of its exact meaning.*

from Part I: A Voyage to Lilliput, Chapter I

1   What became of my companions in the boat, as well as of those who escaped on the rock, or were left in the vessel, I cannot tell; but conclude they were all lost. For my own part, I swam as fortune directed me, and was pushed forward by wind and tide. I often let my legs drop, and could feel no bottom; but when I was almost gone, and able to struggle no longer, I found myself within my depth; and by this time the storm was much abated. The declivity was so small, that I walked near a mile before I got to the shore, which I conjectured was about eight o'clock in the evening. I then advanced forward near half a mile, but could not discover any sign of houses or inhabitants; at least I was in so weak a condition, that I did not observe them. I was extremely tired, and with that, and the heat of the weather, and about half a pint of brandy that I drank as I left the ship, I found myself much inclined to sleep. I lay down on the grass, which was very short and soft, where I slept sounder than ever I remembered to have done in my life, and, as I reckoned, about nine hours; for when I awaked, it was just day-light. I attempted to rise, but was not able to stir: for, as I happened to lie on my back, I found my arms and legs were strongly fastened on each side to the ground; and my hair, which was long and thick, tied down in the same manner. I likewise felt several slender **ligatures** across my body, from my arm-pits to my thighs. I could only look upwards; the sun began to grow hot, and the light offended my eyes.  I heard a confused noise about me; but in the posture I lay, could see nothing except the sky.

2   In a little time I felt something alive moving on my left leg, which advancing gently forward over my breast, came almost up to my chin; when, bending my eyes downwards as much as I could, I perceived it to be a human creature not six inches high, with a bow and arrow in his hands, and a quiver at his back. In the mean time, I felt at least forty more of the same kind (as I

Gulliver held prisoner and tied down by the people of Lilliput, published ca. 1880

NOTES

conjectured) following the first. I was in the utmost astonishment, and roared so loud, that they all ran back in a fright; and some of them, as I was afterwards told, were hurt with the falls they got by leaping from my sides upon the ground. However, they soon returned, and one of them, who ventured so far as to get a full sight of my face, lifting up his hands and eyes by way of admiration, cried out in a shrill but distinct voice, *Hekinah degul*: the others repeated the same words several times, but then I knew not what they meant. I lay all this while, as the reader may believe, in great uneasiness.

3 At length, struggling to get loose, I had the fortune to break the strings, and wrench out the pegs that fastened my left arm to the ground; for, by lifting it up to my face, I discovered the methods they had taken to bind me, and at the same time with a violent pull, which gave me excessive pain, I a little loosened the strings that tied down my hair on the left side, so that I was just able to turn my head about two inches. But the creatures ran off a second time, before I could seize them; whereupon there was a great shout in a very shrill accent, and after it ceased I heard one of them cry aloud *Tolgo phonac;* when in an instant I felt above a hundred arrows **discharged** on my left hand, which, pricked me like so many needles; and besides, they shot another flight into the air, as we do bombs in Europe, whereof many, I suppose, fell on my body, (though I felt them not), and some on my face, which I immediately covered with my left hand. When this shower of arrows was over, I fell a groaning with grief and pain; and then striving again to get loose, they discharged another volley larger than the first, and some of them attempted with spears to stick me in the sides; but by good luck I had on a buff jerkin, which they could not pierce.

4 I thought it the most prudent method to lie still, and my design was to continue so till night, when, my left hand being already loose, I could easily free myself: and as for the inhabitants, I had reason to believe I might be a match for the greatest army they could bring against me, if they were all of the same size with him that I saw. But fortune disposed otherwise of me. When the people observed I was quiet, they discharged no more arrows; but, by the noise I heard, I knew their numbers increased; and about four yards from me, over against my right ear, I heard a knocking for above an hour, like that of people at work; when turning my head that way, as well as the pegs and strings would permit me, I saw a stage erected about a foot and a half from the ground, capable of holding four of the inhabitants, with two or three ladders to mount it: from whence one of them, who seemed to be a person of quality, made me a long speech, whereof I understood not one syllable. But I should have mentioned, that before the principal person began his oration, he cried out three times, *Langro dehul san* (these words and the former were afterwards repeated and explained to me); whereupon, immediately, about fifty of the inhabitants came and cut the strings that fastened the left side of my head, which gave me the liberty of turning it to the right, and of observing

Skill:
Media

*I see a similarity in how both versions poke fun at leaders. The "principal person" in the book and the king in the cartoon both appear to be more concerned with pomp and circumstance than with effective communication.*

the person and gesture of him that was to speak. He appeared to be of a middle age, and taller than any of the other three who attended him, whereof one was a page[1] that held up his train, and seemed to be somewhat longer than my middle finger; the other two stood one on each side to support him. He acted every part of an orator, and I could observe many periods of threatenings, and others of promises, pity, and kindness.

5  I answered in a few words, but in the most submissive manner, lifting up my left hand, and both my eyes to the sun, as calling him for a witness; and being almost famished with hunger, having not eaten a morsel for some hours before I left the ship, I found the demands of nature so strong upon me, that I could not forbear showing my impatience (perhaps against the strict rules of decency) by putting my finger frequently to my mouth, to signify that I wanted food. The *hurgo* (for so they call a great lord, as I afterwards learnt) understood me very well. He descended from the stage, and commanded that several ladders should be applied to my sides, on which above a hundred of the inhabitants mounted and walked towards my mouth, laden with baskets full of meat, which had been provided and sent thither by the king's orders, upon the first intelligence he received of me. I observed there was the flesh of several animals, but could not distinguish them by the taste. There were shoulders, legs, and loins, shaped like those of mutton, and very well dressed, but smaller than the wings of a lark. I ate them by two or three at a mouthful, and took three loaves at a time, about the bigness of musket bullets.

. . .

6  It seems, that upon the first moment I was discovered sleeping on the ground, after my landing, the emperor had early notice of it by an express; and determined in council, that I should be tied in the manner I have related, (which was done in the night while I slept;) that plenty of meat and drink should be sent to me, and a machine prepared to carry me to the capital city.

7  This resolution perhaps may appear very bold and dangerous, and I am confident would not be imitated by any prince in Europe on the like occasion. However, in my opinion, it was extremely **prudent,** as well as generous: for, supposing these people had endeavoured to kill me with their spears and arrows, while I was asleep, I should certainly have awaked with the first sense of smart, which might so far have roused my rage and strength, as to have enabled me to break the strings wherewith I was tied; after which, as they were not able to make resistance, so they could expect no mercy.

. . .

1. **page** a court servant

from Part I: A Voyage to Lilliput, Chapter IV

· · ·

Copyright © BookheadEd Learning, LLC

8   One morning, about a fortnight[2] after I had obtained my liberty, Reldresal, principal secretary (as they style him) for private affairs, came to my house attended only by one servant. He ordered his coach to wait at a distance, and desired I would give him an hours audience; which I readily consented to, on account of his quality and personal merits, as well as of the many good offices he had done me during my solicitations at court. I offered to lie down that he might the more conveniently reach my ear, but he chose rather to let me hold him in my hand during our conversation.

9   He began with compliments on my liberty; said "he might pretend to some merit in it;" but, however, added, "that if it had not been for the present situation of things at court, perhaps I might not have obtained it so soon. For," said he, "as flourishing a condition as we may appear to be in to foreigners, we labour under two mighty evils: a violent faction at home, and the danger of an invasion, by a most potent enemy, from abroad.

10   As to the first, you are to understand, that for about seventy moons past there have been two struggling parties in this empire, under the names of *Tramecksan* and *Slamecksan,* from the high and low heels of their shoes, by which they distinguish themselves. It is alleged, indeed, that the high heels are most agreeable to our ancient constitution; but, however this be, his majesty has determined to make use only of low heels in the administration of the government, and all offices in the gift of the crown, as you cannot but observe; and particularly that his majesty's imperial heels are lower at least by a *drurr* than any of his court (*drurr* is a measure about the fourteenth part of an inch). The **animosities** between these two parties run so high, that they will neither eat, nor drink, nor talk with each other. We compute the *Tramecksan,* or high heels, to exceed us in number; but the power is wholly on our side. We apprehend his imperial highness, the heir to the crown, to have some tendency towards the high heels; at least we can plainly discover that one of his heels is higher than the other, which gives him a hobble in his gait.

11   Now, in the midst of these intestine disquiets, we are threatened with an invasion from the island of Blefuscu, which is the other great empire of the universe, almost as large and powerful as this of his majesty. For as to what we have heard you affirm, that there are other kingdoms and states in the world inhabited by human creatures as large as yourself, our philosophers are in much doubt, and would rather conjecture that you dropped from the

Skill:
Point of View

*The political parties have silly, similar names. Heel height is a significant difference between the parties. This makes me think of political debates I've heard, and it makes me wonder if Swift is being critical of politics.*

---

2. **fortnight** (British) two weeks

NOTES

moon, or one of the stars; because it is certain, that a hundred mortals of your bulk would in a short time destroy all the fruits and cattle of his majesty's dominions: besides, our histories of six thousand moons make no mention of any other regions than the two great empires of Lilliput and Blefuscu. Which two mighty powers have, as I was going to tell you, been engaged in a most obstinate war for six-and-thirty moons past.

12   It began upon the following occasion. It is allowed on all hands, that the primitive way of breaking eggs, before we eat them, was upon the larger end; but his present majesty's grandfather, while he was a boy, going to eat an egg, and breaking it according to the ancient practice, happened to cut one of his fingers. Whereupon the emperor his father published an **edict,** commanding all his subjects, upon great penalties, to break the smaller end of their eggs. The people so highly resented this law, that our histories tell us, there have been six rebellions raised on that account; wherein one emperor lost his life, and another his crown.

13   These civil commotions were constantly fomented by the monarchs of Blefuscu; and when they were quelled, the exiles always fled for refuge to that empire. It is computed that eleven thousand persons have at several times suffered death, rather than submit to break their eggs at the smaller end. Many hundred large volumes have been published upon this controversy: but the books of the Big-endians have been long forbidden, and the whole party rendered incapable by law of holding employments. During the course of these troubles, the emperors of Blefuscu did frequently expostulate by their ambassadors, accusing us of making a schism in religion, by offending against a fundamental doctrine of our great prophet Lustrog, in the fifty-fourth chapter of the Blundecral (which is their Alcoran.)[3]

14   This, however, is thought to be a mere strain upon the text; for the words are these: 'that all true believers break their eggs at the convenient end.' And which is the convenient end, seems, in my humble opinion to be left to every man's conscience, or at least in the power of the chief magistrate to determine. Now, the Big-endian exiles have found so much credit in the emperor of Blefuscu's court, and so much private assistance and encouragement from their party here at home, that a bloody war has been carried on between the two empires for six-and-thirty moons, with various success; during which time we have lost forty capital ships, and a much greater number of smaller vessels, together with thirty thousand of our best seamen and soldiers; and the damage received by the enemy is reckoned to be somewhat greater than ours. However, they have now equipped a numerous fleet, and are just preparing to make a descent upon us; and his imperial majesty, placing great

3. **Alcoran** an archaic name for the Quran, Islam's sacred text

confidence in your valour and strength, has commanded me to lay this account of his affairs before you."

15  I desired the secretary to present my humble duty to the emperor; and to let him know, "that I thought it would not become me, who was a foreigner, to interfere with parties; but I was ready, with the hazard of my life, to defend his person and state against all invaders."

Please note that excerpts and passages in the StudySync® library and this workbook are intended as touchstones to generate interest in an author's work. The excerpts and passages do not substitute for the reading of entire texts, and StudySync® strongly recommends that students seek out and purchase the whole literary or informational work in order to experience it as the author intended. Links to online resellers are available in our digital library. In addition, complete works may be ordered through an authorized reseller by filling out and returning to StudySync® the order form enclosed in this workbook.

# First Read

Read *Gulliver's Travels*. After you read, complete the Think Questions below.

 **THINK QUESTIONS**

1. Why did the small people of Lilliput first try to attack Gulliver but then provide him with food? Use evidence from the text to support your answer.

2. Write two or three sentences describing the two political parties in Lilliput. Be sure to include specific details from the text in your answer.

3. Why does Reldresal believe that his people face "the danger of an invasion" from outside? Cite specific evidence from the text to support your answer.

4. Read the following dictionary entry:

   **discharge**

   dis•charge /dis' CHärj/

   *verb*

   1. to remove or tell someone to leave
   2. to fire or shoot
   3. to relieve oneself of an obligation or duty
   4. to fulfill, perform, or execute a duty

   Which definition most closely matches the meaning of **discharged** as it is used in paragraphs 3 and 4 of the excerpt? Explain why you made this choice.

5. Use the context clues provided in paragraph 10 of the passage to determine the meaning of **animosities.** Write your definition of *animosities* here, and explain how you came to it.

# Skill:
# Point of View

Use the Checklist to analyze Point of View in *Gulliver's Travels*. Refer to the sample student annotations about Point of View in the text.

## ••• CHECKLIST FOR POINT OF VIEW

In order to determine a narrator's point of view through what is directly stated versus what is really meant, note the following:

✓ literary techniques intended to provide humor or criticism. Examples include:

- sarcasm, or the use of language that says one thing but means the opposite

- irony, or a contrast between what one expects to happen and what happens

- understatement, or an instance where a character deliberately makes a situation seem less important or serious than it is

- satire, or the use of humor, irony, exaggeration, or ridicule to expose and criticize people's foolishness or vices

✓ possible critiques an author might be making about contemporary society

✓ an unreliable narrator or character whose point of view cannot be trusted

To analyze a case in which grasping a point of view requires distinguishing what is directly stated in a text from what is really meant, consider the following questions:

✓ How do the cultural lens and experiences of the narrator shape his point of view? How do they shape what he says and how he says it?

✓ Is the narrator reliable? Why?

✓ How does the narrator's point of view contribute to a nonliteral understanding of the text?

✓ How does the use of satire add meaning to the story?

Please note that excerpts and passages in the StudySync® library and this workbook are intended as touchstones to generate interest in an author's work. The excerpts and passages do not substitute for the reading of entire texts, and StudySync® strongly recommends that students seek out and purchase the whole literary or informational work in order to experience it as the author intended. Links to online resellers are available in our digital library. In addition, complete works may be ordered through an authorized reseller by filling out and returning to StudySync® the order form enclosed in this workbook.

Reading & Writing
Companion

37

# Skill:
# Point of View

Reread paragraphs 13 and 14 of *Gulliver's Travels*. Then use the Checklist on the previous page to answer the multiple-choice questions below.

## ⟳ YOUR TURN

1. Which of these quotations most effectively shows how the author uses humor to make the reader think the Lilliputians are foolish?

   ○ A. "These civil commotions were constantly fomented by the monarchs of Blefuscu."
   ○ B. "It is computed that eleven thousand persons have at several times suffered death, rather than submit to break their eggs at the smaller end."
   ○ C. "a bloody war has been carried on between the two empires for six-and-thirty moons"
   ○ D. "However, they have now equipped a numerous fleet, and are just preparing to make a descent upon us."

2. Swift mocks warfare by —

   ○ A. telling how long the war between the empires has lasted.
   ○ B. describing the ships and soldiers employed by each side.
   ○ C. using silly-sounding words to name the countries.
   ○ D. showing that the war began over an ambiguous sentence.

# Skill:
# Media

Use the Checklist to analyze Media in *Gulliver's Travels*. Refer to the sample student annotations about Media in the text.

## ••• CHECKLIST FOR MEDIA

Before analyzing multiple interpretations of a story, drama, or poem, note the following:

✓ similarities and differences in different media, such as the live production of a play or a recorded novel or poetry

✓ the different time periods and cultures in which the source material and interpretations were produced

To analyze multiple interpretations of a story, drama, or poem and evaluate how each version interprets the source text, consider the following questions:

✓ How does each version interpret the source text? What are the main similarities and differences between the two (or more) versions?

✓ In what ways does the medium affect the interpretations of the source text?

✓ If each version is from a different time period and/or culture, what do they reveal about the time period and culture in which they were written?

✓ Does information about the time periods and cultures allow you to make any inferences about the authors' objectives or intentions?

Please note that excerpts and passages in the StudySync® library and this workbook are intended as touchstones to generate interest in an author's work. The excerpts and passages do not substitute for the reading of entire texts, and StudySync® strongly recommends that students seek out and purchase the whole literary or informational work in order to experience it as the author intended. Links to online resellers are available in our digital library. In addition, complete works may be ordered through an authorized reseller by filling out and returning to StudySync® the order form enclosed in this workbook.

Reading & Writing
Companion

39

# Skill:
# Media

Reread paragraph 4 of *Gulliver's Travels,* and compare it with a segment of the *Gulliver's Travels* cartoon. Then use the Checklist on the previous page to answer the multiple-choice questions below.

## ↻ YOUR TURN

1. The book version of *Gulliver's Travels* is more for adults, while the cartoon is more for children. What aspect of the video demonstrates this?

   ○ A. The manner in which Gulliver is restrained

   ○ B. The townspeople's fear of Gulliver

   ○ C. The difference in size between Gulliver and the Lilliputians

   ○ D. The music and sound effects during the battle scene

2. The king in the cartoon displays that he is out of touch with reality when he warns Gulliver, "You'll pay for this!" (2:30), even though he has no way of making Gulliver pay for anything. Which quote from the book suggests a similar avoidance of reality?

   ○ A. "I saw a stage erected about a foot and a half from the ground"

   ○ B. "before the principal person began his oration, he cried out three times, *Langro dehul san*"

   ○ C. "He appeared to be of a middle age, and taller than any of the other three who attended him"

   ○ D. "I could observe many periods of threatenings, and others of promises, pity, and kindness."

# Skill:
# Word Meaning

Use the Checklist to analyze Word Meaning in *Gulliver's Travels*. Refer to the sample student annotations about Word Meaning in the text.

## ••• CHECKLIST FOR WORD MEANING

To find the pronunciation of a word or determine or clarify its precise meaning, do the following:

- ✓ Determine the word's part of speech.

- ✓ Use context clues to make an inferred meaning of the word or phrase.

- ✓ Consult a dictionary to verify your preliminary determination of the meaning of a word or phrase.

- ✓ Decide which definition makes sense within the context of the text.

To determine or clarify a word's part of speech, do the following:

- ✓ Determine what the word is describing.

- ✓ Identify how the word is being used in the phrase or sentence.

To determine or clarify the etymology or standard usage of a word, consider the following questions:

- ✓ How formal or informal is this word?

- ✓ What is the word describing? What inferred meanings can I make?

- ✓ In which context is the word being used?

- ✓ Is this slang? Is it an example of vernacular? In which other contexts might this word be used?

Please note that excerpts and passages in the StudySync® library and this workbook are intended as touchstones to generate interest in an author's work. The excerpts and passages do not substitute for the reading of entire texts, and StudySync® strongly recommends that students seek out and purchase the whole literary or informational work in order to experience it as the author intended. Links to online resellers are available in our digital library. In addition, complete works may be ordered through an authorized reseller by filling out and returning to StudySync® the order form enclosed in this workbook.

Reading & Writing
Companion

41

# Skill:
# Word Meaning

Reread the end of the opening paragraph of Part I of *Gulliver's Travels* and the dictionary entry below to determine the answers to the follow-up questions.

 YOUR TURN

---

**offend** / ə-'fend- /
*transitive verb*

1. a. to break or disregard something, as the law
   b. to cause pain or discomfort to
2. *obsolete:* to cause to sin or fall
3. to cause a person or group to feel angry or upset by something said or done

**Origin:** Middle English *offenden* "to assail, violate, displease, hurt the feelings of," borrowed from Anglo-French and Latin; Anglo-French *offendre,* borrowed from Latin *offendere,* "to strike against, stumble (upon), trouble, break a rule, displease, annoy"

---

1. This question has two parts. First, answer Part A. Then, answer Part B.

   **Part A:** Which definition best fits the way *offended* is used in paragraph 1?

   ○ A. Definition 1.a                    ○ B. Definition 1.b
   ○ C. Definition 2                      ○ D. Definition 3

   **Part B:** Which phrase is a clue to the meaning of the word *offended*?

   ○ A. "several slender ligatures"       ○ B. "heard a confused noise"
   ○ C. "arm-pits to my thighs"           ○ D. "sun began to grow hot"

2. What is the word origin of the word *offend*?

   ○ A. Middle English, Anglo-French, and Latin    ○ B. Latin, French, and Greek
   ○ C. German and Anglo-French                     ○ D. cannot be determined

---

# Close Read

Reread *Gulliver's Travels*. As you reread, complete the Skills Focus questions below. Then use your answers and annotations from the questions to help you complete the Write activity.

## ◎ SKILLS FOCUS

1. Identify a passage that you found funny in Part 1: A Voyage to Lilliput, Chapter 1. Explain what the author's point of view might be in this moment and how it is different from what is directly stated.

2. Identify a passage in which Swift is satirizing society's very narrow understanding of the surrounding world. Explain why his choice to use the Lilliputians to make this point of view clear is effective.

3. In the cartoon you watched, the Lilliputians speak English, whereas in Jonathan Swift's original writing, they speak an unknown language that we read in italics. How does having the Lilliputians speak in a way that you can understand change your experience of the story? In what ways does it deepen your understanding of the text?

4. The word *submit* can have multiple meanings. Read paragraph 13 to see how it is used in this context: "It is computed that eleven thousand persons have at several times suffered death, rather than submit to break their eggs at the smaller end." Given your knowledge of the word, context clues, and the following definition, what do you think is the best interpretation of this word as it is used here? How does the word add humor and a satirical tone to the story?

5. With *Gulliver's Travels,* Jonathan Swift aimed to satirize European leaders by re-creating their ridiculous behaviors in a fantastical setting. In what ways do we see leaders fighting for their ideas in *Gulliver's Travels*? Are these ideas always worth fighting for? Use textual evidence to support your answer.

## ✎ WRITE

PERSONAL RESPONSE: Jonathan Swift's original version of *Gulliver's Travels* is a transparent satire of the European society he lived in. If you were to create a movie version of *Gulliver's Travels* with the purpose of satirizing modern life, what changes would you make to the story? Using what you know about satire and Swift's other satirical works, select one scene you would change. Describe how you would make the movie interpretation of the scene different from the scene in the book to better satirize modern life.

Please note that excerpts and passages in the StudySync® library and this workbook are intended as touchstones to generate interest in an author's work. The excerpts and passages do not substitute for the reading of entire texts, and StudySync® strongly recommends that students seek out and purchase the whole literary or informational work in order to experience it as the author intended. Links to online resellers are available in our digital library. In addition, complete works may be ordered through an authorized reseller by filling out and returning to StudySync® the order form enclosed in this workbook.

Reading & Writing Companion   43

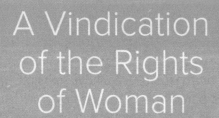

# A Vindication of the Rights of Woman

ARGUMENTATIVE TEXT
Mary Wollstonecraft
1792

## Introduction

Mary Wollstonecraft (1759–1797), a British writer from the 18th century, is considered one of the mothers of the modern feminist movement. Wollstonecraft called for a "revolution in female manners" and for a world in which women were not limited to menial labor and not relegated to the dependent roles of wife, companion, and governess. This excerpt is reproduced from Wollstonecraft's groundbreaking work of feminist philosophy, *A Vindication of the Rights of Woman*.

# "... I wish to persuade women to endeavour to acquire strength, both of mind and body ..."

## from the INTRODUCTION

1    I have turned over various books written on the subject of education, and patiently observed the conduct of parents and the management of schools; but what has been the result? a profound conviction, that the neglected education of my fellow creatures is the grand source of the misery I deplore; and that women in particular, are rendered weak and wretched by a variety of concurring causes, originating from one hasty conclusion. The conduct and manners of women, in fact, evidently prove, that their minds are not in a healthy state; for, like the flowers that are planted in too rich a soil, strength and usefulness are sacrificed to beauty; and the flaunting leaves, after having pleased a fastidious eye, fade, disregarded on the stalk, long before the season when they ought to have arrived at maturity. One cause of this barren blooming I attribute to a false system of education, gathered from the books written on this subject by men, who, considering females rather as women than human creatures, have been more anxious to make them alluring mistresses than rational wives; and the understanding of the sex has been so bubbled by this specious homage, that the civilized women of the present century, with a few exceptions, are only anxious to inspire love, when they ought to cherish a nobler ambition, and by their abilities and virtues exact respect.

...

2    Yet, because I am a woman, I would not lead my readers to suppose, that I mean violently to **agitate** the contested question respecting the equality and inferiority of the sex; but as the subject lies in my way, and I cannot pass it over without subjecting the main tendency of my reasoning to misconstruction, I shall stop a moment to deliver, in a few words, my opinion. In the government of the physical world, it is observable that the female, in general, is inferior to the male. The male pursues, the female yields—this is the law of nature; and it does not appear to be suspended or **abrogated** in favour of woman. This physical superiority cannot be denied—and it is a noble prerogative! But not content with this natural pre-eminence, men endeavour to sink us still lower, merely to render us alluring objects for a moment; and women, intoxicated by

NOTES

Skill: Central or Main Idea

*Wollstonecraft states that she's about to "deliver" her opinion. She probably says this to alert readers that she's about to share her most important views. She says that there is a physical difference between men and women and that society furthers this difference.*

the adoration which men, under the influence of their senses, pay them, do not seek to obtain a durable interest in their hearts, or to become the friends of the fellow creatures who find amusement in their society.

3   I am aware of an obvious inference: from every quarter have I heard exclamations against masculine women; but where are they to be found? If, by this appellation, men mean to **inveigh** against their ardour in hunting, shooting, and gaming, I shall most cordially join in the cry; but if it be, against the imitation of manly virtues, or, more properly speaking, the attainment of those talents and virtues, the exercise of which ennobles the human character, and which raise females in the scale of animal being, when they are comprehensively termed mankind—all those who view them with a philosophical eye must, I should think, wish with me, that they may every day grow more and more masculine.

. . .

4   My own sex, I hope, will excuse me, if I treat them like rational creatures, instead of flattering their fascinating graces, and viewing them as if they were in a state of perpetual childhood, unable to stand alone. I earnestly wish to point out in what true dignity and human happiness consists—I wish to persuade women to endeavour to acquire strength, both of mind and body, and to convince them, that the soft phrases, susceptibility of heart, delicacy of sentiment, and refinement of taste, are almost synonymous with epithets of weakness, and that those beings who are only the objects of pity and that kind of love, which has been termed its sister, will soon become objects of contempt.

5   Dismissing then those pretty feminine phrases, which the men condescendingly use to soften our slavish dependence, and despising that weak elegancy of mind, exquisite sensibility, and sweet docility of manners, supposed to be the sexual characteristics of the weaker vessel, I wish to show that elegance is inferior to virtue, that the first object of laudable ambition is to obtain a character as a human being, regardless of the distinction of sex; and that secondary views should be brought to this simple touchstone.

. . .

6   The education of women has, of late, been more attended to than formerly; yet they are still reckoned a frivolous sex, and ridiculed or pitied by the writers who endeavour by satire or instruction to improve them. It is acknowledged that they spend many of the first years of their lives in acquiring a smattering of accomplishments: meanwhile, strength of body and mind are sacrificed to libertine notions of beauty, to the desire of establishing themselves, the only

way women can rise in the world—by marriage. And this desire making mere animals of them, when they marry, they act as such children may be expected to act: they dress; they paint, and nickname God's creatures. Surely these weak beings are only fit for the seraglio! Can they govern a family, or take care of the poor babes whom they bring into the world?

7    If then it can be fairly deduced from the present conduct of the sex, from the prevalent fondness for pleasure, which takes place of ambition and those nobler passions that open and enlarge the soul; that the instruction which women have received has only tended, with the constitution of civil society, to render them insignificant objects of desire; mere propagators of fools! if it can be proved, that in aiming to accomplish them, without **cultivating** their understandings, they are taken out of their sphere of duties, and made ridiculous and useless when the short lived bloom of beauty is over, I presume that RATIONAL men will excuse me for endeavouring to persuade them to become more masculine and respectable.

8    Indeed, the word *masculine* is only a bugbear. There is little reason to fear that women will acquire too much courage or fortitude, for their apparent inferiority with respect to bodily strength must render them, in some degree, dependent on men in the various relations of life, but why should it be increased by prejudices that give a sex to virtue and confound simple truths with sensual reveries?

from Chapter II: THE PREVAILING OPINION OF A SEXUAL CHARACTER DISCUSSED

9    Consequently, the most perfect education, in my opinion, is such an exercise of the understanding as is best calculated to strengthen the body and form the heart; or, in other words, to enable the individual to attain such habits of virtue as will render it independent. In fact, it is a farce to call any being virtuous whose virtues do not result from the exercise of its own reason. This was Rousseau's[1] opinion respecting men: I extend it to women, and confidently assert that they have been drawn out of their sphere by false refinement, and not by an endeavour to acquire masculine qualities. Still the regal homage which they receive is so intoxicating, that, till the manners of the times are changed, and formed on more reasonable principles, it may be impossible to convince them that the illegitimate power, which they obtain by degrading themselves, is a curse, and that they must return to nature and equality, if they wish to secure the placid satisfaction that unsophisticated affections impart. . . . I may be accused of arrogance; still I must declare, what I firmly believe, that all the writers who have written on the subject of female education and

1.  **Rousseau's** the political philosophies of Jean-Jacques Rousseau (1712–1778) influenced the spread of the Enlightenment and the development of modern political and educational theories

manners, from Rousseau to Dr. Gregory,[2] have contributed to render women more artificial, weaker characters, than they would otherwise have been; and, consequently, more useless members of society. . . .

10  . . . The woman who has only been taught to please, will soon find that her charms are oblique sun-beams, and that they cannot have much effect on her husband's heart when they are seen every day, when the summer is past and gone. . . .

11  Nature has given woman a weaker frame than man; but, to ensure her husband's affections, must a wife, who, by the exercise of her mind and body, whilst she was discharging the duties of a daughter, wife, and mother, has allowed her constitution to retain its natural strength, and her nerves a healthy tone, is she, I say, to condescend, to use art, and feign a sickly delicacy, in order to secure her husband's affection? Weakness may excite tenderness, and gratify the arrogant pride of man; but the lordly caresses of a protector will not gratify a noble mind that pants for and deserves to be respected. Fondness is a poor substitute for friendship!

12  In a seraglio, I grant, that all these arts are necessary; the epicure must have his palate tickled, or he will sink into apathy; but have women so little ambition as to be satisfied with such a condition? Can they supinely dream life away in the lap of pleasure, or in the languor of weariness, rather than assert their claim to pursue reasonable pleasures, and render themselves conspicuous, by practising the virtues which dignify mankind? Surely she has not an immortal soul who can loiter life away, merely employed to adorn her person, that she may amuse the languid hours, and soften the cares of a fellow-creature who is willing to be enlivened by her smiles and tricks, when the serious business of life is over.

13  Besides, the woman who strengthens her body and exercises her mind will, by managing her family and practising various virtues, become the friend, and not the humble dependent of her husband; and if she deserves his regard by possessing such substantial qualities, she will not find it necessary to conceal her affection, nor to pretend to an unnatural coldness of constitution to excite her husband's passions. In fact, if we revert to history, we shall find that the women who have distinguished themselves have neither been the most beautiful nor the most gentle of their sex.

14  Nature, or to speak with strict propriety God, has made all things right; but man has sought him out many inventions to mar the work. I now allude to that part of Dr. Gregory's treatise, where he advises a wife never to let her husband know the extent of her sensibility or affection. Voluptuous precaution; and as

**Skill:**
**Rhetoric**

*Here it seems like the author is appealing to reason. She points out that the logical outcome of more education is that women would be better wives.*

2. **Dr. Gregory** widely regarded Enlightenment-era Scottish writer John Gregory (1724–1773) wrote about morals and manners

ineffectual as absurd. Love, from its very nature, must be transitory. To seek for a secret that would render it constant, would be as wild a search as for the philosopher's stone,[3] or the grand panacea;[4] and the discovery would be equally useless, or rather **pernicious** to mankind. The most holy band of society is friendship. It has been well said, by a shrewd satirist, "that rare as true love is, true friendship is still rarer."

15  This is an obvious truth, and the cause not lying deep, will not elude a slight glance of inquiry.

16  Love, the common passion, in which chance and sensation take place of choice and reason, is in some degree, felt by the mass of mankind; for it is not necessary to speak, at present, of the emotions that rise above or sink below love. This passion, naturally increased by suspense and difficulties, draws the mind out of its accustomed state, and exalts the affections; but the security of marriage, allowing the fever of love to subside, a healthy temperature is thought insipid, only by those who have not sufficient intellect to substitute the calm tenderness of friendship, the confidence of respect, instead of blind admiration, and the sensual emotions of fondness.

17  This is, must be, the course of nature—friendship or indifference inevitably succeeds love. And this constitution seems perfectly to harmonize with the system of government which prevails in the moral world. Passions are spurs to action, and open the mind; but they sink into mere appetites, become a personal momentary gratification, when the object is gained, and the satisfied mind rests in enjoyment. . . .

18  But to view the subject in another point of view. Do passive **indolent** women make the best wives? Confining our discussion to the present moment of existence, let us see how such weak creatures perform their part? Do the women who, by the attainment of a few superficial accomplishments, have strengthened the prevailing prejudice, merely contribute to the happiness of their husbands? Do they display their charms merely to amuse them? And have women, who have early imbibed notions of passive obedience, sufficient character to manage a family or educate children? So far from it, that, after surveying the history of woman, I cannot help agreeing with the severest satirist, considering the sex as the weakest as well as the most oppressed half of the species. . . .

19  But avoiding, as I have hitherto done, any direct comparison of the two sexes collectively, or frankly acknowledging the inferiority of woman, according to the present appearance of things, I shall only insist, that men have increased

3. **philosopher's stone** a mythical substance purported to change any metal into gold or silver, cure all diseases, and grant immortality
4. **panacea** cure-all

that inferiority till women are almost sunk below the standard of rational creatures. Let their faculties have room to unfold, and their virtues to gain strength, and then determine where the whole sex must stand in the intellectual scale. Yet, let it be remembered, that for a small number of distinguished women I do not ask a place.

# First Read

Read *A Vindication of the Rights of Woman*. After you read, complete the Think Questions below.

## ☁ THINK QUESTIONS

1. Who does Wollstonecraft say has written the books about women's education? Why is this detail important to Wollstonecraft's analysis? What inference can readers make based on this detail? Support your answer with evidence from the text.

2. According to Wollstonecraft, what will make women better wives and mothers? What can readers infer about Wollstonecraft's view of marriage based on this idea? Cite evidence from the text to support your response.

3. What can readers infer about Wollstonecraft's ideas about the traditional role of women? Support your response with evidence from the text.

4. Use context to determine the meaning of the word **abrogate** as it is used in *A Vindication of the Rights of Woman*. Write your definition of *abrogate* here, and explain how you determined it.

5. Use context to determine the meaning of the word **indolent** as it is used in *A Vindication of the Rights of Woman*. Write your definition of *indolent* here, and explain how you inferred it.

Please note that excerpts and passages in the StudySync® library and this workbook are intended as touchstones to generate interest in an author's work. The excerpts and passages do not substitute for the reading of entire texts, and StudySync® strongly recommends that students seek out and purchase the whole literary or informational work in order to experience it as the author intended. Links to online resellers are available in our digital library. In addition, complete works may be ordered through an authorized reseller by filling out and returning to StudySync® the order form enclosed in this workbook.

Reading & Writing Companion    51

# Skill:
# Central or Main Idea

Use the Checklist to analyze Central or Main Idea in *A Vindication of the Rights of Woman*. Refer to the sample student annotations about Central or Main Idea in the text.

## ••• CHECKLIST FOR CENTRAL OR MAIN IDEA

To identify two or more central ideas of a text, note the following:

✓ the main idea in each paragraph or group of paragraphs

✓ key details in each paragraph or section of text, distinguishing what they have in common

✓ whether the details contain information that could indicate more than one main idea in a text

- A science text, for example, may provide information about a specific environment and also a message on ecological awareness.

- A biography may contain equally important ideas about a person's achievements, influence, and the time period in which the person lives or lived.

✓ when each central idea emerges

✓ ways the central ideas interact and build on one another

To identify two or more central ideas of a text and analyze their development over the course of the text, including how they interact and build on one another to provide a complex analysis, consider the following questions:

✓ What main idea(s) do the details in each paragraph explain or describe?

✓ What central or main ideas do all the paragraphs support?

✓ How do the central ideas interact and build on one another? How does that affect when they emerge?

✓ How might you provide an objective summary of the text? Which details would you include?

# Skill:
# Central or Main Idea

Reread paragraphs 4 and 5 of *A Vindication of the Rights of Woman*. Then use the Checklist on the previous page to answer the multiple-choice questions below.

## ⟳ YOUR TURN

1. This question has two parts. First, answer Part A. Then, answer Part B.

   **Part A:** Identify the central idea in these paragraphs.

   ○ A. Men often speak to women condescendingly.

   ○ B. Women should work to develop their own characters.

   ○ C. Development of character is important to both men and women.

   ○ D. Women can be treated as rational creatures.

   **Part B:** Which sentence or phrase from the passage best supports the central idea identified in Part A?

   ○ A. "My own sex, I hope, will excuse me, if I treat them like rational creatures, instead of flattering their fascinating graces . . ."

   ○ B. "I wish to persuade women to endeavour to acquire strength, both of mind and body . . ."

   ○ C. "Dismissing then those pretty feminine phrases, which the men condescendingly use to soften our slavish dependence . . ."

   ○ D. "I wish to show that elegance is inferior to virtue . . ."

# Skill:
# Rhetoric

Use the Checklist to analyze Rhetoric in *A Vindication of the Rights of Woman*. Refer to the sample student annotations about Rhetoric in the text.

## ••• CHECKLIST FOR RHETORIC

To identify an author's point of view or purpose in a text, note the following:

✓ the purpose of the text

✓ details and statements that identify the author's point of view or purpose

✓ when the author uses rhetoric to advance their point of view or purpose. Rhetoric is the way in which a writer phrases, or constructs, what they want to say. Writers use many different kinds of rhetorical devices, and the style they employ can contribute to the power, persuasiveness, or beauty of the text. Look for:

- an author's use of sensory language

- words that appeal to the senses, which can create a vivid picture in the minds of readers and listeners and persuade them to accept a specific point of view

- a specific style; for example, the use of assonance or the repetition of certain words can be used to create catchphrases, which can be widely or repeatedly used and easily remembered

✓ when the author's use of rhetoric is particularly effective

To determine an author's point of view or purpose in a text in which the rhetoric is particularly effective, consider the following questions:

✓ Which rhetorical devices can you identify in the text?

✓ How does this writer or speaker use rhetorical devices to persuade an audience?

✓ Do the rhetorical devices work to make the argument or position sound? Why or why not?

✓ How does the use of rhetorical devices affect the way the text is read and understood?

✓ In which way are the rhetorical devices particularly effective?

# Skill:
# Rhetoric

Reread paragraphs 7 and 8 of *A Vindication of the Rights of Woman*. Then use the Checklist on the previous page to answer the multiple-choice questions below.

## ⟳ YOUR TURN

1. This question has two parts. First, answer Part A. Then, answer Part B.

   **Part A:** Which of these is an example of counterargument?

   ○ A. "the instruction which women have received has only tended, with the constitution of civil society, to render them insignificant objects of desire"

   ○ B. "I presume that RATIONAL men will excuse me for endeavoring to persuade them [women] to become more masculine and respectable."

   ○ C. "The word *masculine* is only a bugbear. There is little reason to fear that women will acquire too much courage or fortitude . . ."

   ○ D. " . . . why should it be increased by prejudices that give a sex to virtue and confound simple truths with sensual reveries?"

   **Part B:** Which opposing argument is Wollstonecraft anticipating and addressing with the counterargument in Part A?

   ○ A. Women's education has made them desirable but disrespected.

   ○ B. Men are naturally more rational than women.

   ○ C. Giving women more education will make them too masculine.

   ○ D. Giving women more education will make them less virtuous.

Please note that excerpts and passages in the StudySync® library and this workbook are intended as touchstones to generate interest in an author's work. The excerpts and passages do not substitute for the reading of entire texts, and StudySync® strongly recommends that students seek out and purchase the whole literary or informational work in order to experience it as the author intended. Links to online resellers are available in our digital library. In addition, complete works may be ordered through an authorized reseller by filling out and returning to StudySync® the order form enclosed in this workbook.

Reading & Writing Companion   55

# Close Read

Reread *A Vindication of the Rights of Woman*. As you reread, complete the Skills Focus questions below. Then use your answers and annotations from the questions to help you complete the Write activity.

## ◎ SKILLS FOCUS

1. Identify the key ideas of the first paragraph. Highlight evidence from the text that gives readers clues that help determine the paragraph's main idea.

2. Identify the rhetorical devices the writer uses in paragraph 14, and describe how they develop her main idea.

3. Identify how Wollstonecraft uses rhetoric to appeal to reason and emotion. Highlight at least one example of each.

## ✏ WRITE

RHETORICAL ANALYSIS: Analyze how Mary Wollstonecraft utilizes rhetorical appeals to reason in *A Vindication of the Rights of Woman*. In what ways does she use these appeals to develop her main ideas and challenge pervasive ideas about women's education? Identify specific examples of her rhetorical appeals, and include evidence from the text to support your analysis.

# LITERARY FOCUS:
# Romanticism

## Introduction

This informational text offers historical and cultural background about the society that gave rise to Romanticism. Romantic poets like William Wordsworth, Lord Byron, and John Keats were rejecting ideals of the Enlightenment that emphasized science, order, and modernization, turning instead to the freedom of nature. During the Romantic period, poets wrote of the importance of deep reflection and connection to the natural world. They were daunted by a society in which the Industrial Revolution had engendered deep inequality and poor health. The antidote, Romantic poets proclaimed, was nature.

# "They believed the peacefulness and untouched beauty of the natural world enriched the soul."

NOTES

1   Think of all the technology you use today compared with what your parents had. You can watch movies on a screen that fits in your pocket. You can buy almost any product or service without having to leave your home. You can summon a virtual assistant with a word or phrase. There are so many things you are able to do that your parents could not when they were your age. New technology also creates new problems, however, such as cyberbullying, catfishing, and internet addiction. Some people may even question if all this technology is good for us. This is not the first time people have felt this way. The literary period known as **Romanticism** was born from concerns about modernization, and the movement flourished in the first half of the nineteenth century.

**A Time of Upheaval**

2   The start of the Romantic movement can be traced to the 1798 publication of William Wordsworth's collection of poetry *Lyrical Ballads*, which also includes poems by Samuel Taylor Coleridge. Wordsworth, Coleridge, and other early writers in the movement, such as William Blake, are considered part of the first generation of Romantics. These poets were writing at a time when society was being transformed by two major events: the Industrial Revolution and the Enlightenment. The Industrial Revolution was a transition from an economy based on farming and handmade goods to one based on manufacturing. This change was possible thanks to inventions like steam engines and weaving machines. These developments tended to move people away from nature. People began to leave the countryside and go to the cities, which quickly became overcrowded and polluted. A class of ultra-wealthy industrialists rose to power, while factory workers lived and labored in poor, unsafe, and unhealthful conditions. The Romantic poet Lord Byron, in his narrative poem *The Corsair,* questioned whether the Industrial Revolution really represented progress:

> Such hath it been—shall be—beneath the sun
> The many still must labor for the one.

3   While the Industrial Revolution changed how people lived and worked, the Enlightenment changed how they thought. The Enlightenment was an

Copyright © BookheadEd Learning, LLC

NOTES

*Bridal Procession on the Hardangerfjord*, by
Adolph Tidemand and Hans Gude, 1848

intellectual movement that championed the power of **reason.** People felt empowered to overturn old social structures showed showed skepticism towards religion. They began to replace monarchies with democracies. They believed science and civilization could conquer nature.

4   The Industrial Revolution and the Enlightenment brought many benefits to society, but they also brought problems. Some people worried that the growing gap between humans and the natural world could be harmful. They felt that Enlightenment thinking focused on cold logic and materialism, which they worried would result in the neglect of human emotions and spirit. From these concerns sprang the Romantic movement in arts and letters.

### Nature vs. Science

5   Romantics valued emotions over reason, individualism over **conformity,** and freedom over order. They believed the peacefulness and untouched beauty of the natural world enriched the soul. Not surprisingly, Romanticism contributed to the formation of the environmentalist movement. Although modern environmentalism is connected to fields of science like **ecology** and biology, the Romantics were generally opposed to science, which was seen as an attempt to impose rules and order upon the natural world. Unlike Enlightenment thinkers, who championed the organized garden, Romantics tended to believe that true enlightenment could be found in the wilderness; "civilizing" nature would corrupt it just as civilization can corrupt humanity. As Romantic poet William Wordsworth wrote in "The Tables Turned":

> Our meddling intellect
> Mis-shapes the beauteous forms of things;
> —We murder to dissect.

6   Distrust toward science can also be seen in another work by a famous Romantic writer, Mary Wollstonecraft Shelley's *Frankenstein,* which introduced the character of the "mad scientist" and explored themes of taking science too far.

NOTES

### The Poetic Quest

7 Romanticism prized creativity, and so followers made great contributions to various forms of art. Poetry was particularly esteemed. Wordsworth called poetry a "spontaneous overflow of powerful feelings" and considered it "the language really used" by people. Inspired by the likes of Wordsworth, a younger "second generation" of Romantic poets saw it as their responsibility to guide people in a search for truth and beauty. Percy Bysshe Shelley, husband of Mary Wollstonecraft Shelley, claimed "poets are the unacknowledged legislators of the World." Prominent Romantic poets wrote poems that can be interpreted as allegories for the quest to guide other Romantics. John Keats's poetry is one example of how imagination can allow one to search for beauty and truth without leaving home.

John Keats, a British poet, one of the most important writers of Romanticism

### Romantic Influence in America

8 Romanticism's ideals also found their place among writers in America. At the beginning of the nineteenth century, the newly independent nation was forming its own cultural identity while also expanding westward and investing in urban development. Building on the ideals of its founding documents, American culture, art, philosophy, and literature of the early 1800s focused on individualism, independence, and nature. James Fenimore Cooper, Herman Melville, Henry David Thoreau, and Walt Whitman were among America's Romantic authors. In American literature, additional influences such as puritanism, the practice of slavery, hostility against Native Americans, and the ever-present wilderness of the frontier also affected American Romantics, pushing them to explore the darker truths of their reality and imaginations. Harriet Ann Jacobs, Edgar Allan Poe, and Nathaniel Hawthorne, among others, explored the lived experience of enslavement, the boundaries between the rational and the irrational, the existence of ghosts and monsters, as well as feelings of guilt and aggression.

9 **Major Concepts**

- **The Preeminence of Nature**—As the Industrial Revolution began to transform Britain into a nation of cities and factories, Romantics sought inspiration in the beauty of the natural world, the lives of ordinary workers, and the innocence of childhood. This first generation of Romantic poets included William Wordsworth, William Blake, and Samuel Taylor Coleridge.

- **The Quest for Truth and Beauty**—A second generation of English Romantics inherited many of the enthusiasms and values of their predecessors. During their tragically brief lives, Romantic poets such as Lord Byron, Percy Bysshe Shelley, and John Keats each pursued the ideals of truth and beauty.

**Style and Form**

10 **English Romantic Poetry**

- Although Romantics emphasized emotion and the freedom of the human spirit, they still wrote poetry in a structured poetic form to create meaning.

- Nature was an important feature of Romantic poetry and a source of inspiration.

- Romantic poetry involved **contemplation** and reflection on the part of the speaker.

- Romantic poets often alluded to the art, literature, and culture of the ancient Greeks. Latin classics were a part of the formal education of most Romantics, and many prominent Romantics, such as Samuel Taylor Coleridge, John Keats, and Percy Shelley, all wrote in or translated works from the original Greek.

11 Romanticism can be embodied in the idiom "stop and smell the roses." Modern life can be hectic. Honking traffic and ringing smartphones can make a person feel stressed. Many people benefit from putting aside part of the day for self-reflection and enjoying the outdoors. Romanticism remains popular not only because of the sheer volume of the movement's contributions to art but also because people still need to be reminded not to neglect their emotional well-being. What aspects of modern life do you think Romantics would approve or disapprove of?

# Literary Focus

Read "Literary Focus: Romanticism." After you read, complete the Think Questions below.

 **THINK QUESTIONS**

1. Why were followers of Romanticism unhappy about the Industrial Revolution and the Enlightenment?

2. What might William Wordsworth have meant when he wrote "Our meddling intellect / Mis-shapes the beauteous forms of things; / —We murder to dissect"?

3. How is the Romantic poets' interest in beauty related to other ideas of Romanticism?

4. Use context clues to determine the meaning of the word ***conformity.*** Write your best definition here, along with the words and phrases that were most helpful in determining the word's meaning. Then check a dictionary to confirm your understanding.

5. The word ***ecology*** likely stems from the Greek *oikos*, meaning "house or habitation," and *logos*, meaning "word or account." With this information in mind, write your best definition of the word *ecology* as it is used in this text. Cite any words or phrases that were particularly helpful as you came to your conclusion.

# The Rime of the Ancient Mariner

POETRY
Samuel Taylor Coleridge
1798

## Introduction

"The Rime of the Ancient Mariner" by Samuel Taylor Coleridge (1772–1834) was published in *Lyrical Ballads*, a collaborative collection of poems written with William Wordsworth that helped launch the Romantic movement in England. Coleridge is credited with developing "conversational poetry," in which simple, everyday language is used to convey deep poetic meaning. In "The Rime of the Ancient Mariner," an old sailor detains a reluctant wedding guest and relates a strange, cautionary tale of what happens to those who don't heed omens.

# "Water, water, everywhere, nor any drop to drink."

**Part I**

1   It is an ancient mariner
2   And he stoppeth one of three.
3   —"By thy long grey beard and glittering eye,
4   Now wherefore stoppest thou me?

5   The bridegroom's doors are opened wide,
6   And I am next of kin;
7   The guests are met, the feast is set:
8   May'st hear the merry din."

9   He holds him with his skinny hand,
10  "There was a ship," quoth he.
11  "Hold off! unhand me, grey-beard loon!"
12  Eftsoons[1] his hand dropped he.

13  He holds him with his glittering eye—
14  The wedding-guest stood still,
15  And listens like a three-years' child:
16  The mariner hath his will.

17  The wedding-guest sat on a stone:
18  He cannot choose but hear;
19  And thus spake on that ancient man,
20  The bright-eyed mariner.

21  "The ship was cheered, the harbour cleared,
22  Merrily did we drop
23  Below the kirk,[2] below the hill,
24  Below the lighthouse top.

---

1. **eftsoons** (archaic) afterward
2. **kirk** (Scottish) church

25  The sun came up upon the left,
26  Out of the sea came he!
27  And he shone bright, and on the right
28  Went down into the sea.

29  Higher and higher every day,
30  Till over the mast at noon—"
31  The wedding-guest here beat his breast,
32  For he heard the loud bassoon.

33  The bride hath paced into the hall,
34  Red as a rose is she;
35  Nodding their heads before her goes
36  The merry minstrelsy.

37  The wedding-guest he beat his breast,
38  Yet he cannot choose but hear;
39  And thus spake on that ancient man,
40  The bright-eyed mariner.

41  "And now the storm-blast came, and he
42  Was tyrannous and strong;
43  He struck with his o'ertaking wings,
44  And chased us south along.

45  With sloping masts and dipping prow,
46  As who pursued with yell and blow
47  Still treads the shadow of his foe,
48  And forward bends his head,
49  The ship drove fast, loud roared the blast,
50  And southward aye we fled.

51  Listen, stranger! Mist and snow,
52  And it grew wondrous cold:
53  And ice mast-high came floating by,
54  As green as emerald.

55  And through the drifts the snowy clifts
56  Did send a dismal sheen:
57  Nor shapes of men nor beasts we ken—
58  The ice was all between.

59  The ice was here, the ice was there,
60  The ice was all around:
61  It cracked and growled, and roared and howled,
62  Like noises in a swound!

Please note that excerpts and passages in the StudySync® library and this workbook are intended as touchstones to generate interest in an author's work. The excerpts and passages do not substitute for the reading of entire texts, and StudySync® strongly recommends that students seek out and purchase the whole literary or informational work in order to experience it as the author intended. Links to online resellers are available in our digital library. In addition, complete works may be ordered through an authorized reseller by filling out and returning to StudySync® the order form enclosed in this workbook.

Reading & Writing
Companion

65

NOTES

63   At length did cross an albatross,[3]
64   Thorough the fog it came;
65   As if it had been a Christian soul,
66   We **hailed** it in God's name.

67   It ate the food it ne'er had eat,
68   And round and round it flew.
69   The ice did split with a thunder-fit;
70   The helmsman steered us through!

71   And a good south wind sprung up behind;
72   The albatross did follow,
73   And every day, for food or play,
74   Came to the mariners' hollo![4]

75   In mist or cloud, on mast or shroud,
76   It perched for vespers nine;
77   Whiles all the night, through fog-smoke white,
78   Glimmered the white moon-shine."

79   "God save thee, ancient mariner!
80   From the fiends, that plague thee thus!—
81   Why lookst thou so?" "With my crossbow
82   I shot the albatross.

## Part II

83   The sun now rose upon the right:
84   Out of the sea came he,
85   Still hid in mist, and on the left
86   Went down into the sea.

87   And the good south wind still blew behind,
88   But no sweet bird did follow,
89   Nor any day for food or play
90   Came to the mariners' hollo!

91   And I had done an hellish thing,
92   And it would work 'em woe:
93   For all averred, I had killed the bird
94   That made the breeze to blow.
95   Ah wretch! said they, the bird to slay,
96   That made the breeze to blow!

3. **albatross** a large sea bird
4. **hollo** a shout of excitement and encouragement

97   Nor dim nor red, like God's own head,
98   The glorious sun uprist:
99   Then all averred, I had killed the bird
100  That brought the fog and mist.
101  'Twas right, said they, such birds to slay,
102  That bring the fog and mist.

103  The fair breeze blew, the white foam flew,
104  The furrow followed free;
105  We were the first that ever burst
106  Into that silent sea.

107  Down dropped the breeze, the sails dropped down,
108  'Twas sad as sad could be;
109  And we did speak only to break
110  The silence of the sea!

111  All in a hot and copper sky,
112  The bloody sun, at noon,
113  Right up above the mast did stand,
114  No bigger than the moon.

115  Day after day, day after day,
116  We stuck, nor breath nor motion;
117  As idle as a painted ship
118  Upon a painted ocean.

119  Water, water, everywhere,
120  And all the boards did shrink;
121  Water, water, everywhere,
122  Nor any drop to drink.

123  The very deeps did rot: O Christ!
124  That ever this should be!
125  Yea, slimy things did crawl with legs
126  Upon the slimy sea.

127  About, about, in reel and rout
128  The death-fires danced at night;
129  The water, like a witch's oils,
130  Burnt green, and blue and white.

131  And some in dreams assured were
132  Of the spirit that plagued us so;
133  Nine fathom deep he had followed us
134  From the land of mist and snow.

135 And every tongue, through utter drought,
136 Was withered at the root;
137 We could not speak, no more than if
138 We had been choked with soot.

139 Ah! wel-a-day! what evil looks
140 Had I from old and young!
141 Instead of the cross, the albatross
142 About my neck was hung.

**Part III**

143 There passed a weary time. Each throat
144 Was parched, and glazed each eye.
145 A weary time! A weary time!
146 How glazed each weary eye,
147 When looking westward, I beheld
148 A something in the sky.

149 At first it seemed a little speck,
150 And then it seemed a mist;
151 It moved and moved, and took at last
152 A certain shape, I wist.

153 A speck, a mist, a shape, I wist!
154 And still it neared and neared:
155 As if it dodged a water sprite,
156 It plunged and tacked and veered.

157 With throats unslaked, with black lips baked,
158 We could nor laugh nor wail;
159 Through utter drouth all dumb we stood!
160 I bit my arm, I sucked the blood,
161 And cried, A sail! a sail!

162 With throats unslaked, with black lips baked,
163 Agape they heard me call:
164 Gramercy! they for joy did grin,
165 And all at once their breath drew in,
166 As they were drinking all.

167 See! see! (I cried) she tacks no more!
168 Hither to work us weal;
169 Without a breeze, without a tide,
170 She steadies with upright keel!

171    The western wave was all aflame.
172    The day was well nigh done!
173    Almost upon the western wave
174    Rested the broad bright sun;
175    When that strange shape drove suddenly
176    Betwixt us and the sun.

177    And straight the sun was flecked with bars,
178    (Heaven's mother send us grace!)
179    As if through a dungeon grate he peered
180    With broad and burning face.

181    Alas! (thought I, and my heart beat loud)
182    How fast she nears and nears!
183    Are those her sails that glance in the sun,
184    Like restless gossameres?

185    Are those her ribs through which the sun
186    Did peer, as through a grate?
187    And is that woman all her crew?
188    Is that a Death? and are there two?
189    Is Death that woman's mate?

190    Her lips were red, her looks were free,
191    Her locks were yellow as gold:
192    Her skin was as white as leprosy,
193    The nightmare Life-in-Death was she,
194    Who thicks man's blood with cold.

195    The naked hulk alongside came,
196    And the twain were casting dice;
197    'The game is done! I've won! I've won!'
198    Quoth she, and whistles thrice.

199    The sun's rim dips; the stars rush out:
200    At one stride comes the dark;
201    With far-heard whisper, o'er the sea,
202    Off shot the spectre bark.

203    We listened and looked sideways up!
204    Fear at my heart, as at a cup,
205    My lifeblood seemed to sip!
206    The stars were dim, and thick the night,
207    The steersman's face by his lamp gleamed white;
208    From the sails the dews did drip—
209    Till clomb above the eastern bar

 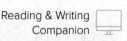

210  The horned moon, with one bright star
211  Within the nether tip.

212  One after one, by the star-dogged moon,
213  Too quick for groan or sigh,
214  Each turned his face with ghastly pang,
215  And cursed me with his eye.

216  Four times fifty living men,
217  (And I heard nor sigh nor groan)
218  With heavy thump, a lifeless lump,
219  They dropped down one by one.

220  Their souls did from their bodies fly—
221  They fled to bliss or woe!
222  And every soul, it passed me by,
223  Like the whizz of my crossbow!"

## Part IV

224  "I fear thee, ancient mariner!
225  I fear thy skinny hand!
226  And thou art long, and lank, and brown,
227  As is the ribbed sea-sand.

228  I fear thee and thy glittering eye,
229  And thy skinny hand, so brown."—
230  "Fear not, fear not, thou wedding-guest!
231  This body dropped not down.

232  Alone, alone, all, all alone,
233  Alone on a wide wide sea!
234  And never a saint took pity on
235  My soul in agony.

236  The many men, so beautiful!
237  And they all dead did lie:
238  And a thousand thousand slimy things
239  Lived on; and so did I.

240  I looked upon the rotting sea,
241  And drew my eyes away;
242  I looked upon the rotting deck,
243  And there the dead men lay.

244 I looked to heaven, and tried to pray;
245 But or ever a prayer had gushed,
246 A wicked whisper came, and made
247 My heart as dry as dust.

248 I closed my lids, and kept them close,
249 Till the balls like pulses beat;
250 For the sky and the sea, and the sea and the sky
251 Lay like a load on my weary eye,
252 And the dead were at my feet.

253 The cold sweat melted from their limbs,
254 Nor rot nor reek did they:
255 The look with which they looked on me
256 Had never passed away.

257 An orphan's curse would drag to hell
258 A spirit from on high;
259 But oh! more horrible than that
260 Is the curse in a dead man's eye!
261 Seven days, seven nights, I saw that curse,
262 And yet I could not die.

263 The moving moon went up the sky,
264 And nowhere did **abide:**
265 Softly she was going up,
266 And a star or two beside—

267 Her beams bemocked the sultry main,
268 Like April hoar-frost spread;
269 But where the ship's huge shadow lay,
270 The charmed water burnt alway
271 A still and awful red.

272 Beyond the shadow of the ship,
273 I watched the water snakes:
274 They moved in tracks of shining white,
275 And when they reared, the elfish[5] light
276 Fell off in hoary flakes.

277 Within the shadow of the ship
278 I watched their rich attire:
279 Blue, glossy green, and velvet black,
280 They coiled and swam; and every track
281 Was a flash of golden fire.

---

5. **elfish** relating to characteristics of an elf or elves

NOTES

282   O happy living things! No tongue
283   Their beauty might declare:
284   A spring of love gushed from my heart,
285   And I blessed them unaware:
286   Sure my kind saint took pity on me,
287   And I blessed them unaware.

288   The selfsame moment I could pray;
289   And from my neck so free
290   The albatross fell off, and sank
291   Like lead into the sea.

## Part V

292   Oh sleep! it is a gentle thing,
293   Beloved from pole to pole!
294   To Mary-Queen the praise be given!
295   She sent the gentle sleep from heaven,
296   That slid into my soul.

297   The silly buckets on the deck,
298   That had so long remained,
299   I dreamt that they were filled with dew;
300   And when I awoke, it rained.

301   My lips were wet, my throat was cold,
302   My garments all were dank;
303   Sure I had drunken in my dreams,
304   And still my body drank.

305   I moved, and could not feel my limbs:
306   I was so light—almost
307   I thought that I had died in sleep,
308   And was a blessed ghost.

309   And soon I heard a roaring wind:
310   It did not come anear;
311   But with its sound it shook the sails,
312   That were so thin and sere.

313   The upper air bursts into life!
314   And a hundred fire-flags sheen,
315   To and fro they were hurried about!
316   And to and fro, and in and out,
317   The wan stars danced between.

Copyright © BookheadEd Learning, LLC

318 And the coming wind did roar more loud,
319 And the sails did sigh like sedge;
320 And the rain poured down from one black cloud;
321 The moon was at its edge.

322 The thick black cloud was cleft, and still
323 The moon was at its side:
324 Like waters shot from some high crag,
325 The lightning fell with never a jag,
326 A river steep and wide.

327 The loud wind never reached the ship,
328 Yet now the ship moved on!
329 Beneath the lightning and the moon
330 The dead men gave a groan.

331 They groaned, they stirred, they all uprose,
332 Nor spake, nor moved their eyes;
333 It had been strange, even in a dream,
334 To have seen those dead men rise.

335 The helmsman steered, the ship moved on;
336 Yet never a breeze up-blew;
337 The mariners all 'gan work the ropes,
338 Where they were wont to do;
339 They raised their limbs like lifeless tools—
340 We were a ghastly crew.

341 The body of my brother's son
342 Stood by me, knee to knee:
343 The body and I pulled at one rope,
344 But he said nought to me."

345 "I fear thee, ancient mariner!"
346 "Be calm, thou wedding-guest!
347 'Twas not those souls that fled in pain,
348 Which to their corses came again,
349 But a troop of spirits blessed.

350 For when it dawned—they dropped their arms,
351 And clustered round the mast;
352 Sweet sounds rose slowly through their mouths,
353 And from their bodies passed.

NOTES

354   Around, around, flew each sweet sound,
355   Then darted to the sun;
356   Slowly the sounds came back again,
357   Now mixed, now one by one.

358   Sometimes a-dropping from the sky
359   I heard the skylark sing;
360   Sometimes all little birds that are,
361   How they seemed to fill the sea and air
362   With their sweet jargoning!

363   And now 'twas like all instruments,
364   Now like a lonely flute;
365   And now it is an angel's song,
366   That makes the heavens be mute.

367   It ceased; yet still the sails made on
368   A pleasant noise till noon,
369   A noise like of a hidden brook
370   In the leafy month of June,

371   That to the sleeping woods all night
372   Singeth a quiet tune.

373   Till noon we silently sailed on,
374   Yet never a breeze did breathe:
375   Slowly and smoothly went the ship,
376   Moved onward from beneath.

377   Under the keel nine fathom deep,
378   From the land of mist and snow,
379   The spirit slid: and it was he
380   That made the ship to go.
381   The sails at noon left off their tune,
382   And the ship stood still also.

383   The sun, right up above the mast,
384   Had fixed her to the ocean:
385   But in a minute she 'gan stir,
386   With a short uneasy motion—
387   Backwards and forwards half her length
388   With a short uneasy motion.

389   Then like a pawing horse let go,
390   She made a sudden bound:

391  It flung the blood into my head,
392  And I fell down in a swound.

393  How long in that same fit I lay,
394  I have not to declare;
395  But ere my living life returned,
396  I heard and in my soul discerned
397  Two voices in the air.

398  'Is it he?' quoth one, 'Is this the man?
399  By him who died on cross,
400  With his cruel bow he laid full low
401  The harmless albatross.

402  The spirit who bideth by himself
403  In the land of mist and snow,
404  He loved the bird that loved the man
405  Who shot him with his bow.'

406  The other was a softer voice,
407  As soft as honeydew:
408  Quoth he, 'The man hath penance done,
409  And penance more will do.'

## Part VI

### FIRST VOICE

410  'But tell me, tell me! speak again,
411  Thy soft response renewing—
412  What makes that ship drive on so fast?
413  What is the ocean doing?'

### SECOND VOICE

414  'Still as a slave before his lord,
415  The ocean hath no blast;
416  His great bright eye most silently
417  Up to the moon is cast—

418  If he may know which way to go;
419  For she guides him smooth or grim.
420  See, brother, see! how graciously
421  She looketh down on him.'

NOTES

### FIRST VOICE

422 'But why drives on that ship so fast,
423 Without or wave or wind?'

### SECOND VOICE

424 'The air is cut away before,
425 And closes from behind.

426 Fly, brother, fly! more high, more high!
427 Or we shall be belated:
428 For slow and slow that ship will go,
429 When the mariner's trance is **abated.**'

430 I woke, and we were sailing on
431 As in a gentle weather:
432 'Twas night, calm night, the moon was high;
433 The dead men stood together.

434 All stood together on the deck,
435 For a charnel-dungeon fitter:
436 All fixed on me their stony eyes,
437 That in the moon did glitter.

438 The pang, the curse, with which they died,
439 Had never passed away:
440 I could not draw my eyes from theirs,
441 Nor turn them up to pray.

442 And now this spell was snapped: once more
443 I viewed the ocean green,
444 And looked far forth, yet little saw
445 Of what had else been seen—

446 Like one, that on a lonesome road
447 Doth walk in fear and dread,
448 And having once turned round walks on,
449 And turns no more his head;
450 Because he knows a frightful fiend
451 Doth close behind him tread.

452 But soon there breathed a wind on me,
453 Nor sound nor motion made:
454 Its path was not upon the sea,
455 In ripple or in shade.

 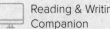

NOTES

456 It raised my hair, it fanned my cheek
457 Like a meadow-gale of spring—
458 It mingled strangely with my fears,
459 Yet it felt like a welcoming.

460 Swiftly, swiftly flew the ship,
461 Yet she sailed softly too:
462 Sweetly, sweetly blew the breeze—
463 On me alone it blew.

464 O dream of joy! is this indeed
465 The lighthouse top I see?
466 Is this the hill? is this the kirk?
467 Is this mine own country?

468 We drifted o'er the harbour bar,
469 And I with sobs did pray—
470 O let me be awake, my God!
471 Or let me sleep alway!

472 The harbour bay was clear as glass,
473 So smoothly it was strewn!
474 And on the bay the moonlight lay,
475 And the shadow of the moon.

476 The rock shone bright, the kirk no less,
477 That stands above the rock:
478 The moonlight steeped in silentness
479 The steady weathercock.

480 And the bay was white with silent light,
481 Till rising from the same,
482 Full many shapes, that shadows were,
483 In crimson colours came.

484 A little distance from the prow
485 Those crimson shadows were:
486 I turned my eyes upon the deck—
487 O Christ! what saw I there!

488 Each corse lay flat, lifeless and flat,
489 And, by the holy rood!
490 A man all light, a **seraph** man,
491 On every corse there stood.

Please note that excerpts and passages in the StudySync® library and this workbook are intended as touchstones to generate interest in an author's work. The excerpts and passages do not substitute for the reading of entire texts, and StudySync® strongly recommends that students seek out and purchase the whole literary or informational work in order to experience it as the author intended. Links to online resellers are available in our digital library. In addition, complete works may be ordered through an authorized reseller by filling out and returning to StudySync® the order form enclosed in this workbook.

Reading & Writing
Companion

77

NOTES

492  This seraph band, each waved his hand:
493  It was a heavenly sight!
494  They stood as signals to the land,
495  Each one a lovely light;

496  This seraph band, each waved his hand,
497  No voice did they impart—
498  No voice; but oh! the silence sank
499  Like music on my heart.

500  But soon I heard the dash of oars,
501  I heard the pilot's cheer;
502  My head was turned perforce away
503  And I saw a boat appear.

504  The pilot and the pilot's boy,
505  I heard them coming fast:
506  Dear Lord in heaven! it was a joy
507  The dead men could not blast.

508  I saw a third—I heard his voice:
509  It is the hermit good!
510  He singeth loud his godly hymns
511  That he makes in the wood.
512  He'll shrieve my soul, he'll wash away
513  The albatross's blood.

## Part VII

514  This hermit good lives in that wood
515  Which slopes down to the sea.
516  How loudly his sweet voice he rears!
517  He loves to talk with mariners
518  That come from a far country.

519  He kneels at morn, and noon, and eve—
520  He hath a cushion plump:
521  It is the moss that wholly hides
522  The rotted old oak stump.

523  The skiff boat neared: I heard them talk,
524  'Why, this is strange, I trow!
525  Where are those lights so many and fair,
526  That signal made but now?'

NOTES

527  'Strange, by my faith!' the hermit said—
528  'And they answered not our cheer!
529  The planks look warped! and see those sails,
530  How thin they are and sere!
531  I never saw aught like to them,
532  Unless perchance it were

533  Brown skeletons of leaves that lag
534  My forest-brook along;
535  When the ivy tod is heavy with snow,
536  And the owlet whoops to the wolf below,
537  That eats the she-wolf's young.'

538  'Dear Lord! it hath a fiendish look,'
539  The pilot made reply,
540  'I am a-feared'—'Push on, push on!'
541  Said the hermit cheerily.

542  The boat came closer to the ship,
543  But I nor spake nor stirred;
544  The boat came close beneath the ship,
545  And straight a sound was heard.

546  Under the water it rumbled on,
547  Still louder and more dread:
548  It reached the ship, it split the bay;
549  The ship went down like lead.

550  Stunned by that loud and dreadful sound,
551  Which sky and ocean smote
552  Like one that hath been seven days drowned
553  My body lay afloat;
554  But swift as dreams, myself I found
555  Within the pilot's boat.

556  Upon the whirl, where sank the ship,
557  The boat spun round and round;
558  And all was still, save that the hill
559  Was telling of the sound.

560  I moved my lips—the pilot shrieked
561  And fell down in a fit;
562  The holy hermit raised his eyes,
563  And prayed where he did sit.

Please note that excerpts and passages in the StudySync® library and this workbook are intended as touchstones to generate interest in an author's work. The excerpts and passages do not substitute for the reading of entire texts, and StudySync® strongly recommends that students seek out and purchase the whole literary or informational work in order to experience it as the author intended. Links to online resellers are available in our digital library. In addition, complete works may be ordered through an authorized reseller by filling out and returning to StudySync® the order form enclosed in this workbook.

Reading & Writing
Companion

79

564    I took the oars: the pilot's boy,
565    Who now doth crazy go,
566    Laughed loud and long, and all the while
567    His eyes went to and fro.
568    'Ha! ha!' quoth he, 'full plain I see,
569    The devil knows how to row.'

570    And now, all in my own country,
571    I stood on the firm land!
572    The hermit stepped forth from the boat,
573    And scarcely he could stand.

574    'Oh shrieve me, shrieve me, holy man!'
575    The hermit crossed his brow.
576    'Say quick,' quoth he, 'I bid thee say—
577    What manner of man art thou?'

578    Forthwith this frame of mine was wrenched
579    With a woeful agony,
580    Which forced me to begin my tale;
581    And then it left me free.

582    Since then, at an uncertain hour,
583    That agony returns:
584    And till my ghastly tale is told,
585    This heart within me burns.

586    I pass, like night, from land to land;
587    I have strange power of speech;
588    The moment that his face I see,
589    I know the man that must hear me:
590    To him my tale I teach.

591    What loud uproar bursts from that door!
592    The wedding-guests are there:
593    But in the garden-bower the bride
594    And bridemaids singing are:
595    And hark the little vesper bell,
596    Which biddeth me to prayer!

597    O wedding-guest! This soul hath been
598    Alone on a wide wide sea:
599    So lonely 'twas, that God himself
600    Scarce seemed there to be.

601 Oh sweeter than the marriage feast,
602 'Tis sweeter far to me,
603 To walk together to the kirk
604 With a goodly company!—

605 To walk together to the kirk,
606 And all together pray,
607 While each to his great Father bends,
608 Old men, and babes, and loving friends
609 And youths and maidens gay!

610 Farewell, farewell! but this I tell
611 To thee, thou wedding-guest!
612 He prayeth well, who loveth well
613 Both man and bird and beast.

614 He prayeth best, who loveth best
615 All things both great and small;
616 For the dear God who loveth us,
617 He made and loveth all."

618 The mariner, whose eye is bright,
619 Whose beard with age is hoar,
620 Is gone: and now the wedding-guest
621 Turned from the bridegroom's door.

622 He went like one that hath been stunned,
623 And is of sense **forlorn:**
624 A sadder and a wiser man,
625 He rose the morrow morn.

---

## ✏ WRITE

EXPLANATORY: In "The Rime of the Ancient Mariner," the aging mariner stops a young man on his way to a wedding party and shares with him a cautionary tale. Explain why the mariner is compelled to repeat his story. What is he trying to discharge by retelling it? Will he succeed? Use evidence from the text to support your response.

Please note that excerpts and passages in the StudySync® library and this workbook are intended as touchstones to generate interest in an author's work. The excerpts and passages do not substitute for the reading of entire texts, and StudySync® strongly recommends that students seek out and purchase the whole literary or informational work in order to experience it as the author intended. Links to online resellers are available in our digital library. In addition, complete works may be ordered through an authorized reseller by filling out and returning to StudySync® the order form enclosed in this workbook.

Reading & Writing
Companion

81

# Snake

POETRY
D. H. Lawrence
1923

## Introduction

D. H. Lawrence (1885–1930), an English novelist and poet, authored works that were banned in the U.S. until the 1960s due to their controversial content. He is best known for his criticism of industrialized society and his reverence for nature. "Snake," from *Birds, Beasts and Flowers*, tells the story of a boy who encounters a snake at a water trough. The boy's internal struggle with how to treat the snake mirrors one of Lawrence's literary preoccupations—exploring human beings' relationship to the natural world.

# "And yet those voices: /
## *If you were not afraid, you would kill him!"*

1   A snake came to my water-trough
2   On a hot, hot day, and I in pajamas for the heat,
3   To drink there.
4   In the deep, strange-scented shade of the great dark carob-tree
5   I came down the steps with my pitcher
6   And must wait, must stand and wait, for there he was at the trough before me.

7   He reached down from a fissure in the earth-wall in the gloom
8   And trailed his yellow-brown slackness soft-bellied down, over the edge of
      the stone trough
9   And rested his throat upon the stone bottom,
10  And where the water had dripped from the tap, in a small clearness,
11  He sipped with his straight mouth,
12  Softly drank through his straight gums, into his **slack** long body,
13  Silently.

14  Someone was before me at my water-trough,
15  And I, like a second comer, waiting.

16  He lifted his head from his drinking, as cattle do,
17  And looked at me vaguely, as drinking cattle do,
18  And flickered his two-forked tongue from his lips, and mused a moment,
19  And stooped and drank a little more,
20  Being earth-brown, earth-golden from the burning bowels of the earth
21  On the day of Sicilian July, with Etna[1] smoking.

22  The voice of my education said to me
23  He must be killed,
24  For in Sicily the black, black snakes are innocent, the gold are venomous.

25  And voices in me said, If you were a man
26  You would take a stick and break him now, and finish him off.

---

1. **Etna** a volcano on the island of Sicily that has long been active

27   But I must confess how I liked him,
28   How glad I was he had come like a guest in quiet, to drink at my
     water-trough
29   And depart peaceful, **pacified,** and thankless,
30   Into the burning bowels of this earth?

31   Was it cowardice, that I dared not kill him? Was it perversity, that I longed to
     talk to him? Was it humility, to feel so honoured?
32   I felt so honoured.

33   And yet those voices:
34   *If you were not afraid, you would kill him!*

35   And truly I was afraid, I was most afraid,
36   But even so, honoured still more
37   That he should seek my hospitality
38   From out the dark door of the secret earth.

39   He drank enough
40   And lifted his head, dreamily, as one who has drunken,
41   And flickered his tongue like a forked night on the air, so black,
42   Seeming to lick his lips,
43   And looked around like a god, unseeing, into the air,
44   And slowly turned his head,
45   And slowly, very slowly, as if thrice a dream,
46   **Proceeded** to draw his slow length curving round
47   And climb again the broken bank of my wall-face.

48   And as he put his head into that dreadful hole,
49   And as he slowly drew up, snake-easing his shoulders, and entered farther,
50   A sort of horror, a sort of protest against his withdrawing into that horrid
     black hole,
51   Deliberately going into the blackness, and slowly drawing himself after,
52   Overcame me now his back was turned.

53   I looked round, I put down my pitcher,
54   I picked up a clumsy log
55   And threw it at the water-trough with a clatter.

56   I think it did not hit him,
57   But suddenly that part of him that was left behind convulsed in undignified
     haste,
58   Writhe'd like lightning, and was gone
59   Into the black hole, the earth-lipped fissure in the wall-front,
60   At which, in the intense still noon, I stared with fascination.

61   And immediately I regretted it.

62   I thought how **paltry,** how vulgar, what a mean act!

63   I despised myself and the voices of my accursed human education.

64   And I thought of the albatross,

65   And I wished he would come back, my snake.

66   For he seemed to me again like a king,

67   Like a king in exile, uncrowned in the underworld,

68   Now due to be crowned again.

69   And so, I missed my chance with one of the lords

70   Of life.

71   And I have something to **expiate:**

72   A pettiness.

---

### ✏ WRITE

PERSONAL RESPONSE: In the poem "Snake," D. H. Lawrence explores the theme of societal expectations when he writes, "And yet those voices: / *If you were not afraid, you would kill him*!" Reflect on a time in your life when you felt pressured to act a certain way. Write about your experience, and relate it to the speaker's experience in Lawrence's poem. Include evidence from the text, as well as details from your personal experience, to develop your essay.

# Preface to *Lyrical Ballads*

INFORMATIONAL TEXT
William Wordsworth
1800

## Introduction

William Wordsworth (1770–1850), one of the foremost English poets of the Romantic period, was best known for his exploration of the human relationship to nature and the self. The poetry collection *Lyrical Ballads* was published in 1798 with contributions from fellow Romantic poet Samuel Taylor Coleridge and is widely considered to mark the beginning of the Romantic movement. The following text was included as part of the preface to the second edition of *Lyrical Ballads*, published in 1800. In the preface, Wordsworth outlines their poetic principles and makes the case for a different kind of poetry.

# "... all good poetry is the spontaneous overflow of powerful feelings ..."

NOTES

preface to the 1800 edition

1   ... The principal object then which I proposed to myself in these Poems was to make the incidents of common life interesting by tracing in them, truly though not ostentatiously, the primary laws of our nature: chiefly as far as regards the manner in which we associate ideas in a state of excitement. Low and **rustic** life was generally chosen because in that situation the essential passions of the heart find a better soil in which they can attain their maturity, are less under restraint, and speak a plainer and more emphatic language; because in that situation our elementary feelings exist in a state of greater simplicity and consequently may be more accurately contemplated and more forcibly communicated; because the manners of rural life germinate from those elementary feelings; and from the necessary character of rural occupations are more easily comprehended; and are more durable; and lastly, because in that situation the passions of men are incorporated with the beautiful and permanent forms of nature. The language too of these men is adopted (purified indeed from what appear to be its real defects, from all lasting and rational causes of dislike or disgust) because such men hourly communicate with the best objects from which the best part of language is originally derived; and because, from their rank in society and the sameness and narrow circle of their intercourse, being less under the action of social vanity they convey their feelings and notions in simple and unelaborated expressions. Accordingly such a language arising out of repeated experience and regular feelings is a more permanent and a far more philosophical language than that which is frequently substituted for it by Poets, who think that they are **conferring** honour upon themselves and their art in proportion as they separate themselves from the sympathies of men, and indulge in **arbitrary** and capricious habits of expression in order to furnish food for fickle tastes and fickle appetites of their own creation.

2   I cannot be **insensible** of the present outcry against the triviality and meanness both of thought and language, which some of my contemporaries have occasionally introduced into their metrical compositions; and I acknowledge that this defect where it exists, is more dishonorable to the Writer's own character than false refinement or arbitrary innovation, though I should

NOTES

contend at the same time that it is far less pernicious in the sum of its consequences. From such verses the Poems in these volumes will be found distinguished at least by one mark of difference, that each of them has a worthy *purpose*. Not that I mean to say that I always began to write with a distinct purpose formally conceived; but I believe that my habits of meditation have so formed my feelings, as that my descriptions of such objects as strongly excite those feelings, will be found to carry along with them a *purpose*. If in this opinion I am mistaken I can have little right to the name of a Poet. For all good poetry is the spontaneous overflow of powerful feelings; but though this be true, Poems to which any value can be attached, were never produced on any variety of subjects but by a man who being possessed of more than usual organic sensibility had also thought long and deeply. For our continued influxes of feeling are modified and directed by our thoughts, which are indeed the representatives of all our past feelings; and as by contemplating the relation of these general representatives to each other, we discover what is really important to men, so by the repetition and continuance of this act, feelings connected with important subjects will be nourished, till at length, if we be originally possessed of much organic sensibility, such habits of mind will be produced that by obeying blindly and mechanically the impulses of those habits we shall describe objects and utter sentiments of such a nature and in such connection with each other, that the understanding of the being to whom we address ourselves, if he be in a healthful state of association, must necessarily be in some degree enlightened, his taste exalted, and his affections **ameliorated.**

## ✏ WRITE

EXPLANATORY: Wordsworth's preface to *Lyrical Ballads* explains how his approach to poetry departs from earlier styles. Summarize his approach and how he contrasts it with other styles of poetry, using evidence from the text. Do you agree with Wordsworth? Why or why not?

# Lines Composed a Few Miles above Tintern Abbey

**POETRY**
William Wordsworth
1798

## Introduction

William Wordsworth (1770–1850) gave "Lines Composed a Few Miles above Tintern Abbey, On Revisiting the Banks of the Wye during a Tour. July 13, 1798" one of literature's most specific titles, recalling his thoughts at a particular place that left a deep impression on him—the banks of the Wye River near Wales. It was a place of peace in a life sometimes troubled by tragedy: the early death of both parents, the loss of two young children, and his separation from his beloved sister, to whom the poem is addressed. Meditating on the natural world around Tintern Abbey, Wordsworth also explores the way nature can soothe the soul in a world growing ever busier and less peaceful.

# O sylvan Wye! thou wanderer thro' the woods, / How often has my spirit turned to thee!

**Skill: Figurative Language**

*The speaker repeats* length *and* long *using hyperbole to describe how difficult it is has been to be away from this place.*

*Soft inland murmur is a sensory metaphor suggesting that the sounds of nature are calling to the speaker.*

1  Five years have past; five summers, with the length
2  Of five long winters! and again I hear
3  These waters, rolling from their mountain-springs
4  With a soft inland murmur.—Once again
5  Do I behold these steep and lofty cliffs,
6  That on a wild secluded scene impress
7  Thoughts of more deep seclusion; and connect
8  The landscape with the quiet of the sky.
9  The day is come when I again **repose**
10  Here, under this dark sycamore, and view
11  These plots of cottage-ground, these orchard-tufts,
12  Which at this season, with their unripe fruits,
13  Are clad in one green hue, and lose themselves
14  'Mid groves and copses. Once again I see
15  These hedge-rows, hardly hedge-rows, little lines
16  Of sportive wood run wild: these pastoral farms,
17  Green to the very door; and wreaths of smoke
18  Sent up, in silence, from among the trees!
19  With some uncertain notice, as might seem
20  Of vagrant dwellers in the houseless woods,
21  Or of some Hermit's cave, where by his fire
22  The Hermit sits alone.

23  These beauteous forms,
24  Through a long absence, have not been to me
25  As is a landscape to a blind man's eye:
26  But oft, in lonely rooms, and 'mid the din
27  Of towns and cities, I have owed to them,
28  In hours of weariness, sensations sweet,
29  Felt in the blood, and felt along the heart;
30  And passing even into my purer mind
31  With **tranquil** restoration:—feelings too
32  Of unremembered pleasure: such, perhaps,

David Cox, *Tintern Abbey, Monmouthshire* circa 1840.

Copyright © BookheadEd Learning, LLC

33  As have no slight or trivial influence

34  On that best portion of a good man's life,

35  His little, nameless, unremembered, acts

36  Of kindness and of love. Nor less, I trust,

37  To them I may have owed another gift,

38  Of aspect more sublime; that blessed mood,

39  In which the burthen of the mystery,

40  In which the heavy and the weary weight

41  Of all this unintelligible world,

42  Is lightened:—that serene and blessed mood,

43  In which the affections gently lead us on,—

44  Until, the breath of this corporeal frame

45  And even the motion of our human blood

46  Almost suspended, we are laid asleep

47  In body, and become a living soul:

48  While with an eye made quiet by the power

49  Of harmony, and the deep power of joy,

50  We see into the life of things.

51  If this

52  Be but a vain belief, yet, oh! how oft—

53  In darkness and amid the many shapes

54  Of joyless daylight; when the fretful stir

55  Unprofitable, and the fever of the world,

56  Have hung upon the beatings of my heart—

57  How oft, in spirit, have I turned to thee,

58  O **sylvan**[1] Wye![2] thou wanderer thro' the woods,

59  How often has my spirit turned to thee!

60  And now, with gleams of half-extinguished thought,

61  With many recognitions dim and faint,

62  And somewhat of a sad perplexity,

63  The picture of the mind revives again:

64  While here I stand, not only with the sense

65  Of present pleasure, but with pleasing thoughts

66  That in this moment there is life and food

67  For future years. And so I dare to hope,

68  Though changed, no doubt, from what I was when first

69  I came among these hills; when like a roe

70  I bounded o'er the mountains, by the sides

71  Of the deep rivers, and the lonely streams,

72  Wherever nature led: more like a man

73  Flying from something that he dreads, than one

74  Who sought the thing he loved. For nature then

Skill:
Context Clues

*Burthen* is preceded by the article *the* and followed by the preposition *of*, so it is probably a noun.

The repetition of *in which* suggests that "burthen of the mystery" is related to "the heavy and the weary weight."

---

1  **sylvan**  related to woods or forests

2. **Wye**  the river along whose banks William Wordsworth walked during his visit

NOTES

75 (The coarser pleasures of my boyish days
76 And their glad animal movements all gone by)
77 To me was all in all.—I cannot paint
78 What then I was. The sounding **cataract**[3]
79 Haunted me like a passion: the tall rock,
80 The mountain, and the deep and gloomy wood,
81 Their colours and their forms, were then to me
82 An appetite; a feeling and a love,
83 That had no need of a remoter charm,
84 By thought supplied, not any interest
85 Unborrowed from the eye.—That time is past,
86 And all its aching joys are now no more,
87 And all its dizzy raptures. Not for this
88 Faint[4] I, nor mourn nor murmur; other gifts
89 Have followed; for such loss, I would believe,
90 Abundant recompense. For I have learned
91 To look on nature, not as in the hour
92 Of thoughtless youth; but hearing oftentimes
93 The still sad music of humanity,
94 Nor harsh nor grating, though of ample power

**Skill: Figurative Language**

The speaker uses contradictory language, describing a positive feeling, "joy" as something "that disturbs." Wordsworth uses a paradox to illustrate the intense impact that nature has on him.

95 To chasten and **subdue.**—And I have felt
96 A presence that disturbs me with the joy
97 Of elevated thoughts; a sense sublime
98 Of something far more deeply interfused,
99 Whose dwelling is the light of setting suns,
100 And the round ocean and the living air,
101 And the blue sky, and in the mind of man:
102 A motion and a spirit, that impels
103 All thinking things, all objects of all thought,
104 And rolls through all things. Therefore am I still
105 A lover of the meadows and the woods
106 And mountains; and of all that we behold
107 From this green earth; of all the mighty world
108 Of eye, and ear,—both what they half create,
109 And what perceive; well pleased to recognise
110 In nature and the language of the sense
111 The anchor of my purest thoughts, the nurse,
112 The guide, the guardian of my heart, and soul
113 Of all my moral being.

114 Nor perchance,
115 If I were not thus taught, should I the more
116 Suffer my genial spirits to decay:

---

3 **cataract** a waterfall
4. **faint** to lose heart; to become depressed

117  For thou art with me here upon the banks
118  Of this fair river; thou my dearest Friend,
119  My dear, dear Friend; and in thy voice I catch
120  The language of my former heart, and read
121  My former pleasures in the shooting lights
122  Of thy wild eyes. Oh! yet a little while
123  May I behold in thee what I was once,
124  My dear, dear Sister! and this prayer I make,
125  Knowing that Nature never did betray,
126  The heart that loved her; 'tis her privilege,
127  Through all the years of this our life, to lead
128  From joy to joy: for she can so inform
129  The mind that is within us, so impress
130  With quietness and beauty, and so feed
131  With lofty thoughts, that neither evil tongues,
132  Rash judgments, nor the sneers of selfish men,
133  Nor greetings where no kindness is, nor all
134  The dreary intercourse of daily life,
135  Shall e'er prevail against us, or disturb
136  Our cheerful faith, that all which we behold
137  Is full of blessings. Therefore let the moon
138  Shine on thee in thy solitary walk; And let the misty mountain-winds be free
139  To blow against thee: and, in after years,
140  When these wild ecstasies shall be matured
141  Into a sober pleasure; when thy mind
142  Shall be a mansion for all lovely forms,
143  Thy memory be as a dwelling-place
144  For all sweet sounds and harmonies; oh! Then,
145  If solitude, or fear, or pain, or grief,
146  Should be thy portion, with what healing thoughts
147  Of tender joy wilt thou remember me,
148  And these my exhortations! Nor, perchance—
149  If I should be where I no more can hear
150  Thy voice, nor catch from thy wild eyes these gleams
151  Of past existence—wilt thou then forget
152  That on the banks of this delightful stream
153  We stood together; and that I, so long
154  A worshipper of Nature, hither came
155  Unwearied in that service: rather say
156  With warmer love—oh! with far deeper zeal
157  Of holier love. Nor wilt thou then forget,
158  That after many wanderings, many years
159  Of absence, these steep woods and lofty cliffs,
160  And this green pastoral landscape, were to me
161  More dear, both for themselves and for thy sake!

LINES COMPOSED A FEW
MILES ABOVE TINTERN ABBEY

# First Read

Read "Lines Composed a Few Miles above Tintern Abbey." After you read, complete the Think Questions below.

 THINK QUESTIONS

1. What is the effect of the opening eight lines of the poem in light of the poem's title? In what way do these lines clarify the author's relationship to the countryside around Tintern Abbey? Explain, using textual evidence to support your answer.

2. Based on the second stanza, did the speaker in the poem forget the countryside around Tintern Abbey when he was away from it? Explain, using textual evidence to support your answer.

3. In the third stanza, the author mentions "the fretful stir / Unprofitable, and the fever of the world." What is he referring to with these words? Cite any other relevant quotes or passages from the poem in your answer.

4. In describing the beauties of nature in the fourth stanza, the author mentions "deep rivers, and the lonely streams" as well as the "sounding cataract." Using context clues, define **cataract.** Write your definition here, and explain how you inferred it.

5. Use context clues to determine the definition of **subdue** as it is used in the poem. Write your definition of *subdue* here, and explain how you inferred it.

# Skill:
# Context Clues

Use the Checklist to analyze Context Clues in "Lines Composed a Few Miles above Tintern Abbey." Refer to the sample student annotations about Context Clues in the text.

## ••• CHECKLIST FOR CONTEXT CLUES

To use context as a clue to the meaning of a word or phrase, note the following:

- ✓ clues about the word's part of speech
- ✓ clues in the surrounding text about the word's meaning
- ✓ words with similar denotations that seem to differ slightly in meaning
- ✓ signal words that cue a type of context clue, such as:
  - *comparably*, *related to*, or *similarly* to signal a comparison context clue
  - *on the other hand*, *however*, or *in contrast* to signal a contrast context clue
  - *by reason of*, *because*, or *as a result* to signal a cause-and-effect context clue

To determine the meaning of a word or phrase as it is used in a text, consider the following questions:

- ✓ What is the meaning of the overall sentence, paragraph, or text?
- ✓ How does the position of the word in the sentence help me define it?
- ✓ How does the word function in the sentence? Which clues help identify the word's part of speech?
- ✓ Which clues in the text suggest the word's definition?
- ✓ What do I think the word means?

To verify the preliminary determination of the meaning of the word or phrase based on context, consider the following questions:

- ✓ Does the definition I inferred make sense within the context of the sentence?
- ✓ Which of the dictionary's definitions makes sense within the context of the sentence?

Please note that excerpts and passages in the StudySync® library and this workbook are intended as touchstones to generate interest in an author's work. The excerpts and passages do not substitute for the reading of entire texts, and StudySync® strongly recommends that students seek out and purchase the whole literary or informational work in order to experience it as the author intended. Links to online resellers are available in our digital library. In addition, complete works may be ordered through an authorized reseller by filling out and returning to StudySync® the order form enclosed in this workbook.

Reading & Writing Companion

95

## Skill:
## Context Clues

Reread lines 115–138 of "Lines Composed a Few Miles above Tintern Abbey." Then use the Checklist on the previous page to answer the multiple-choice questions below.

**YOUR TURN**

1. Which clues could you use to accurately determine the part of speech of the word *former*?

   ○ A. *Former* is used twice to modify the verbs the speaker uses, such as *catch* and *read*. It must be an adverb.

   ○ B. *Former* is used twice following the pronoun *my,* suggesting that the speaker possesses it. It must be a noun.

   ○ C. *Former* is used twice, once to describe *heart* and once to describe *pleasures*. It must be an adjective.

   ○ D. *Former* is used twice following the pronoun *my* and to describe *wild eyes*. It must be an adjective.

2. This question has two parts. First, answer Part A. Then, answer Part B.

   **Part A:** Based on context clues in the poem, what is most likely the meaning of the word *former*?

   ○ A. Something that is now destroyed or has changed form

   ○ B. A person that forms, or makes, something

   ○ C. Something that in the past used to have a particular role

   ○ D. A frame or core around which an electrical coil can be wound

   **Part B:** Which line from the poem best supports the answer to Part A?

   ○ A. "Of this fair river; thou my dearest Friend,"

   ○ B. "My dear, dear Friend; and in thy voice I catch"

   ○ C. "Of thy wild eyes. Oh! yet a little while"

   ○ D. "May I behold in thee what I was once,"

# Skill:
# Figurative Language

Use the Checklist to analyze Figurative Language in "Lines Composed a Few Miles above Tintern Abbey." Refer to the sample student annotations about Figurative Language in the text.

## ••• CHECKLIST FOR FIGURATIVE LANGUAGE

To determine the meaning of a figure of speech in context, note the following:

✓ words that mean one thing literally and suggest something else

✓ similes, metaphors, or personification

✓ figures of speech, including

- paradoxes, or a seemingly contradictory statement that when further investigated or explained proves to be true, such as:

  > a character described as "a wise fool"

  > a character stating "I must be cruel to be kind."

- hyperboles, or exaggerated statements not meant to be taken literally, such as:

  > a child saying "I'll be doing this homework until I'm one hundred!"

  > a claim such as, "I'm so hungry I could eat a horse!"

- sensory metaphors, or comparisons that emphasize the senses, such as:

  > a character being compared to a light: "When she walked in, she lit up the entire room."

  > a place described using language related to taste: "The visit to the restaurant was bittersweet."

To interpret a figure of speech in context and analyze its role in the text, consider the following questions:

✓ Where is a figure of speech or figurative language in the text, and what seems to be the purpose of it?

✓ What impact does exaggeration or hyperbole have on your understanding of the text?

✓ How does the figurative language develop the message or theme?

Please note that excerpts and passages in the StudySync® library and this workbook are intended as touchstones to generate interest in an author's work. The excerpts and passages do not substitute for the reading of entire texts, and StudySync® strongly recommends that students seek out and purchase the whole literary or informational work in order to experience it as the author intended. Links to online resellers are available in our digital library. In addition, complete works may be ordered through an authorized reseller by filling out and returning to StudySync® the order form enclosed in this workbook.

Reading & Writing Companion

97

# Skill:
# Figurative Language

Reread lines 64–95 of "Lines Composed a Few Miles above Tintern Abbey." Then use the Checklist on the previous page to answer the multiple-choice questions below.

## ⟳ YOUR TURN

1.  The author uses references to animals in phrases such as "like a roe," "bounded o'er the mountains," and "glad animal movements" to—

    ○ A.  suggest that the speaker used to enjoy watching the movements of the animals in their natural environment, and that he continues to enjoy it during this second visit.

    ○ B.  convey that in his youth, the speaker experienced nature in the way an animal lives in the natural world, with feeling and instinct rather than intellectual thought.

    ○ C.  express a negative tone about the behaviors of boyhood, which can be immature and superficial compared to the way the speaker is now approaching nature.

    ○ D.  help readers understand that the speaker, now more mature, wishes he still had the ability to live comfortably in nature, as animals do.

2.  The speaker says that he now has "other gifts." His use of the phrases "hearing oftentimes / The still sad music of humanity, / Nor harsh nor grating . . ." is an effective description of one of these gifts because it—

    ○ A.  suggests in a positive way that although the speaker has matured, he still has the views of nature he held as a youth.

    ○ B.  emphasizes the viewpoint that humanity, like nature, is at times cruel and disagreeable, but yet should be viewed as a gift.

    ○ C.  conveys that the speaker believes that a sense of harmony between nature and humanity is impossible.

    ○ D.  shows that the speaker has gained a deeper appreciation of nature, one in which he recognizes a connection between nature and one's spiritual life.

3. Identify the paradox from the statements below.

○ A. "And all its aching joys are now no more,"

○ B. "Wherever nature led: more like a man"

○ C. "Have followed; for such loss, I would believe,"

○ D. "An appetite; a feeling and a love,"

LINES COMPOSED A FEW
MILES ABOVE TINTERN ABBEY

# Close Read

Reread "Lines Composed a Few Miles above Tintern Abbey." As you reread, complete the Skills Focus questions below. Then use your answers and annotations from the questions to help you complete the Write activity.

## ◎ SKILLS FOCUS

1. Find an example of imagery that reflects the thoughts and feelings of the speaker. Use context clues to determine the nuanced meaning of the image.

2. Choose a passage that helps you visualize the landscape. Explain how the descriptions and sensory metaphors deepen your understanding of the message of the poem.

3. Locate an example of figurative language, such as hyperbole, paradox, metaphor, or simile, in the poem. Explain how it contributes to the overall meaning of the poem.

4. Consider the principles of plain language and rustic simplicity that Wordsworth outlines in his preface to *Lyrical Ballads*. Identify examples of each in "Lines Composed a Few Miles above Tintern Abbey," and describe how they represent Wordsworth's ideas.

5. Throughout the poem, the speaker experiences nature while also remembering his youth. What effect do the memories of younger days have on the poem? What is the power of this story over the speaker's current experience?

## ✏ WRITE

LITERARY ANALYSIS: The essence of Romantic poetry is the precise choice of language that invokes the emotional response of the individual in relation to nature. Wordsworth revolutionized the literary form by exploiting the power of words to reveal the emotional depth of everyday experiences. Write an essay in which you analyze and evaluate Wordsworth's use of figurative language to contribute to the poem's message and emotional effect. Use context clues to analyze language and ideas that might be challenging.

Copyright © BookheadEd Learning, LLC

# Letters of John Keats

INFORMATIONAL TEXT
John Keats
1817–1818

## Introduction

John Keats (1795–1821) was a poet and writer of letters during the Romantic literary tradition in England. During his lifetime, he was criticized for his lack of classical education and considered an outsider. He originally studied to become a surgeon, but he gave up medicine to become a poet. He died tragically of tuberculosis at the young age of 25 after publishing only 54 poems. Today, he is considered one of the greatest English poets. These three selections from Keats's letters to his friends and family, written in 1817 and 1818, provide insight into his artistic ideals.

# "... if poetry comes not as naturally as the leaves to a tree, it had better not come at all."

1 —TO GEORGE AND THOMAS KEATS

2 Hampstead, December 22, 1817.

3 My dear Brothers—I must crave your pardon for not having written ere this. . . . I spent Friday evening with Wells and went next morning to see *Death on the Pale horse*. It is a wonderful picture, when West's age is considered; but there is nothing to be **intense** upon, no women one feels mad to kiss, no face swelling into reality. The excellence of every art is its intensity, capable of making all disagreeables evaporate from their being in close relationship with Beauty and Truth—Examine King Lear,[1] and you will find this exemplified throughout; but in this picture we have unpleasantness without any momentous depth of speculation excited, in which to bury its repulsiveness— The picture is larger than Christ rejected.

4 I dined with Haydon the Sunday after you left, and had a very pleasant day, I dined too (for I have been out too much lately) with Horace Smith and met his two Brothers with Hill and Kingston and one Du Bois, they only served to convince me how superior humour is to wit, in respect to enjoyment—These men say things which make one start, without making one feel, they are all alike; their manners are alike; they all know fashionables; they have all a mannerism in their very eating and drinking, in their mere handling a Decanter. They talked of Kean and his low company—would I were with that company instead of yours said I to myself! I know such like acquaintance will never do for me and yet I am going to Reynolds, on Wednesday. Brown and Dilke walked with me and back from the Christmas pantomime. I had not a dispute, but a disquisition, with Dilke upon various subjects; several things dove-tailed in my mind, and at once it struck me what quality went to form a Man of Achievement, especially in Literature, and which Shakespeare possessed so enormously—I mean *Negative Capability*, that is, when a man is capable of being in uncertainties, mysteries, doubts, without any irritable reaching after fact and reason. Coleridge, for instance, would let go by a fine isolated

---

1. **King Lear** William Shakespeare's famous tragedy *King Lear* traces the calamitous downfall of its titular monarch

NOTES

**verisimilitude** caught from the Penetralium of mystery, from being incapable of remaining content with half-knowledge. This pursued through volumes would perhaps take us no further than this, that with a great poet the sense of Beauty overcomes every other consideration, or rather obliterates all consideration.

. . .

5   —TO JOHN TAYLOR

6   Hampstead, February 27, 1818.

. . .

7   In poetry I have a few axioms,[2] and you will see how far I am from their centre.

8   1st. I think poetry should surprise by a fine **excess,** and not by singularity; It should strike the reader as a wording of his own highest thoughts, and appear almost a remembrance.

9   2d. Its touches of beauty should never be half-way, thereby making the reader breathless, instead of content. The rise, the progress, the setting of Imagery should, like the sun, come natural to him, shine over him, and set soberly, although in magnificence, leaving him in the luxury of twilight. But it is easier to think what poetry should be, than to write it—

10   And this leads me to another axiom—That if poetry comes not as naturally as the leaves to a tree, it had better not come at all.

. . .

11   —TO J. H. REYNOLDS

12   Teignmouth, May 3rd, 1818.

. . .

13   And to be more explicit and to show you how tall I stand by the giant, I will put down a simile of human life as far as I now perceive it; that is, to the point to which I say we both have arrived at—Well—I compare human life to a large Mansion of Many Apartments, two of which I can only describe, the doors of the rest being as yet shut upon me—The first we step into we call the infant or thoughtless Chamber, in which we remain as long as we do not think—We remain there a long while, and **notwithstanding** the doors of the second Chamber remain wide open, showing a bright appearance, we care not to hasten to it; but are at length imperceptibly impelled by the awakening of the

2. **axioms** widely known facts or truths

NOTES

thinking principle—within us—we no sooner get into the second Chamber, which I shall call the Chamber of Maiden-Thought, than we become intoxicated with the light and the atmosphere, we see nothing but pleasant wonders, and think of delaying there for ever in delight: However among the effects this breathing is father of is that tremendous one of sharpening one's vision into the heart and nature of Man—of convincing ones nerves that the World is full of Misery and Heartbreak, Pain, Sickness, and oppression—whereby This Chamber of Maiden Thought becomes gradually darken'd and at the same time on all sides of it many doors are set open—but all dark—all leading to dark passages—We see not the balance of good and evil. We are in a Mist— *We* are now in that state—We feel the 'burden of the Mystery,' To this point was Wordsworth come, as far as I can **conceive** when he wrote 'Tintern Abbey' and it seems to me that his Genius is explorative of those dark Passages. Now if we live, and go on thinking, we too shall explore them. He is a Genius and superior to us, in so far as he can, more than we, make discoveries, and shed a light in them—Here I must think Wordsworth is deeper than Milton, though I think it has depended more upon the general and gregarious advance of intellect, than individual greatness of Mind . . .

## ✏ WRITE

CORRESPONDENCE: In his personal correspondence, Keats frequently comments on the artistic works of others. Write your own letter to a friend in which you react to an artistic inspiration. It could be a painting, movie, book, or even the style of a fashion icon. Be sure to explain your source of inspiration and describe how it has influenced you.

# Ode on a Grecian Urn

POETRY
John Keats
1820

## Introduction

What is the relationship between art and life, between beauty and truth? The Romantic poet John Keats (1795–1821) lived to be only 25 years old, having grown up in England and dying from tuberculosis in a bedroom that overlooked the Piazza di Spagna in Rome. "Ode on a Grecian Urn" was written only a year before his death, and like much of Keats's work, it examines the relationships between life, death, beauty, and truth with depth and lyrical insight

# "More happy love! more happy, happy love!"

**Skill: Poetic Elements and Structure**

*In the tradition of odes, the speaker uses formal language to address the urn directly. This formal language indicates a serious tone.*

1   Thou still unravish'd bride of quietness,
2   Thou **foster**-child of silence and slow time,
3   **Sylvan** historian, who canst thus express
4   A flowery tale more sweetly than our rhyme:
5   What leaf-fring'd legend haunts about thy shape
6   Of deities or mortals, or of both,
7   In Tempe[1] or the dales of Arcady?[2]
8   What men or gods are these? What maidens loth?
9   What mad pursuit? What struggle to escape?
10   What pipes and timbrels? What wild ecstasy?

11   Heard melodies are sweet, but those unheard
12   Are sweeter; therefore, ye soft pipes, play on;
13   Not to the sensual ear, but, more endear'd,
14   Pipe to the spirit ditties of no tone:
15   Fair youth, beneath the trees, thou canst not leave
16   Thy song, nor ever can those trees be bare;
17   Bold Lover, never, never canst thou kiss,
18   Though winning near the goal—yet, do not grieve;
19   She cannot fade, though thou hast not thy bliss,
20   For ever wilt thou love, and she be fair!

21   Ah, happy, happy boughs! that cannot shed
22   Your leaves, nor ever bid the Spring adieu;
23   And, happy melodist, unwearied,
24   For ever piping songs for ever new;
25   More happy love! more happy, happy love!
26   For ever warm and still to be enjoy'd,
27   For ever panting, and for ever young;
28   All breathing human passion far above,
29   That leaves a heart high-sorrowful and cloy'd,
30   A burning forehead, and a parching tongue.

Ancient Greek urn

1. **Tempe** a beautiful valley in Arcadia
2. **Arcady** Arcadia, a mountainous region in Greece, traditionally considered an ideal rustic landscape

NOTES

31  Who are these coming to the sacrifice?
32  To what green altar, O mysterious priest,
33  Lead'st thou that heifer lowing at the skies,
34  And all her silken flanks with garlands drest?
35  What little town by river or sea shore,
36  Or mountain-built with peaceful citadel,
37  Is emptied of this folk, this pious morn?
38  And, little town, thy streets for evermore
39  Will silent be; and not a soul to tell
40  Why thou art **desolate,** can e'er return.

41  O Attic shape![3] Fair attitude! with brede
42  Of marble men and maidens overwrought,
43  With forest branches and the trodden weed;
44  Thou, silent form, dost tease us out of thought
45  As doth eternity: Cold **Pastoral!**
46  When old age shall this **generation** waste,
47  Thou shalt remain, in midst of other woe
48  Than ours, a friend to man, to whom thou say'st,
49  "Beauty is truth, truth beauty,"—that is all
50  Ye know on earth, and all ye need to know.

3 **Attic shape**  in the simple, graceful style characteristic of Attica, the region in Greece where Athens is located

# First Read

Read "Ode on a Grecian Urn." After you read, complete the Think Questions below.

 THINK QUESTIONS

1. In the first stanza of the poem, what is it that can express "A flowery tale more sweetly than our rhyme"?

2. In the second stanza, Keats writes of the "Bold Lover" who can never kiss his beloved. Why, according to the poem, should he not grieve?

3. In what sense is the urn "a friend to man"? Explain what Keats means by this phrase, using textual evidence from the poem to support your response.

4. Use context clues to determine the meaning of the word **sylvan** as it is used in stanza 1. Write your definition of *sylvan* here, and explain which clues helped you determine the word's meaning.

5. Read the following dictionary entry:

**desolate**

des•o•late /ˈde-sə-lət, ˈde-zə-/

*adjective*

a. lacking the items that make people feel welcome in a place

b. very lonely and sad

c. (of a place) deserted and bleak

Which of these definitions most closely matches the meaning of **desolate** as it is used in stanza 4? Write the correct definition of *desolate* here, and explain which clues helped you choose it.

# Skill:
# Poetic Elements and Structure

Use the Checklist to analyze Poetic Elements and Structure in "Ode on a Grecian Urn." Refer to the sample student annotations about Poetic Elements and Structure in the text.

## ••• CHECKLIST FOR POETIC ELEMENTS AND STRUCTURE

In order to analyze a poet's choices concerning how to structure specific parts of a poem, note the following:

✓ the form and overall structure of the poem

✓ the rhyme, rhythm, and meter, if present

✓ lines and stanzas in the poem that suggest its meanings and aesthetic impact

✓ how the poet began or ended the poem

✓ if the poet provided a comedic or tragic resolution

✓ poetic terminology, such as the following:

- **ode:** a type of lyric poem that is serious with an elevated tone and style that usually celebrates a person, a quality, or an object, or expresses a private meditation

- **apostrophe:** a figure of speech in which an idea, personified object, or absent person is directly addressed (Nearly all odes include an apostrophe.)

- **elegy:** a poem that laments a death or some other great loss

To analyze how an author's choices concerning how to structure specific parts of a poem contribute to its overall structure and meaning as well as its aesthetic impact, consider the following questions:

✓ How does the poet structure the poem? What is the structure of specific parts?

✓ How do the poet's choices contribute to the poem's overall structure, meaning, and aesthetic impact?

✓ How does the poem reflect a specific literary time period and culture?

✓ How is this poem different from the poetry of other literary time periods and cultures?

Please note that excerpts and passages in the StudySync® library and this workbook are intended as touchstones to generate interest in an author's work. The excerpts and passages do not substitute for the reading of entire texts, and StudySync® strongly recommends that students seek out and purchase the whole literary or informational work in order to experience it as the author intended. Links to online resellers are available in our digital library. In addition, complete works may be ordered through an authorized reseller by filling out and returning to StudySync® the order form enclosed in this workbook.

Reading & Writing Companion

109

# Skill:
# Poetic Elements and Structure

Reread lines 41–50 of "Ode on a Grecian Urn." Then use the Checklist on the previous page to answer the multiple-choice questions below.

## ⟳ YOUR TURN

1. Identify Keats's use of *chiasmus* in the excerpt. Chiasmus is a device in which words, grammatical constructions, or concepts are repeated in reverse order for rhetorical or literary effect.

   ○ A. "O Attic shape! Fair attitude!"

   ○ B. "With forest branches and the trodden weed;"

   ○ C. "As doth eternity: Cold Pastoral!"

   ○ D. "'Beauty is truth, truth beauty,'"

2. What is the effect of chiasmus in the excerpt?

   ○ A. To highlight words that are important to the poem's overall meaning

   ○ B. To de-emphasize the importance of beauty in the poem

   ○ C. To explain that the urn's beauty will eventually fade

   ○ D. To keep with the poem's regular rhyme scheme

# Close Read

Reread "Ode on a Grecian Urn." As you reread, complete the Skills Focus questions below. Then use your answers and annotations from the questions to help you complete the Write activity.

## ◎ SKILLS FOCUS

1. Identify figurative language the poet uses to describe the urn in the first stanza. What does this example of figurative language reveal about the speaker's view of the urn?

2. Notice all the question marks and the repetition of the word *What* in the first stanza. What is the effect of the poet's choice to structure the stanza this way? What does this structure suggest about the urn?

3. Highlight a section of the second stanza of "Ode on a Grecian Urn" that describes the difference between heard and unheard music. Explain how this distinction helps develop the poem's theme.

4. Identify a section of the fifth stanza that focuses on the passage of time, and explain how this section reflects the poem's theme.

5. In "Ode on a Grecian Urn," the speaker views three different stories on an urn, and each has a different emotional impact. What is the power of these stories over the speaker? Support your answer with textual evidence.

## ✏ WRITE

LITERARY ANALYSIS: "Ode on a Grecian Urn" is a famous ode devoted to an ancient Greek urn. Write an essay that analyzes how Keats uses figurative language as well as poetic elements and structure to express ideas about art, culture, and society. Support your analysis with textual evidence from the poem.

Please note that excerpts and passages in the StudySync® library and this workbook are intended as touchstones to generate interest in an author's work. The excerpts and passages do not substitute for the reading of entire texts, and StudySync® strongly recommends that students seek out and purchase the whole literary or informational work in order to experience it as the author intended. Links to online resellers are available in our digital library. In addition, complete works may be ordered through an authorized reseller by filling out and returning to StudySync® the order form enclosed in this workbook.

Reading & Writing Companion   111

# Ozymandias

POETRY
Percy Bysshe Shelley
1818

studysync tv

## Introduction

Percy Bysshe Shelley (1792–1822) was known for his radical ideas and unconventional lifestyle. Like *Frankenstein*, which was written by his second wife, Mary Shelley, the poem "Ozymandias" was composed in response to a challenge. Shelley and his friend poet Horace Smith submitted poems to *The Examiner* on the occasion of the statue of Pharaoh Ramses II being transported from Egypt to London. Shelley's 14-line sonnet appeared in the paper first in January 1818. The imaginative poet invented a traveler and a sculptor's inscription, evoking the ancient relic's ruin as a metaphor for the fall of dynasties and the limitations of tyrants.

# "Look on my works, ye Mighty, and despair!"

1  I met a traveller from an antique land
2  Who said: 'Two vast and trunkless legs of stone
3  Stand in the desert. Near them, on the sand,
4  Half sunk, a shattered **visage** lies, whose frown,
5  And wrinkled lip, and sneer of cold command,
6  Tell that its sculptor well those passions read
7  Which yet survive, stamped on these lifeless things,
8  The hand that **mocked** them and the heart that fed.
9  And on the **pedestal** these words appear—
10 "My name is Ozymandias, king of kings:
11 Look on my works, ye Mighty, and **despair!**"
12 Nothing beside remains. Round the decay
13 Of that **colossal** wreck, boundless and bare
14 The lone and level sands stretch far away.

Sandstone statue of Ramses II, displayed in the Nubian Museum in Aswan, Egypt

Shelley, Percy Bysshe. "Ozymandias." *The Examiner*, 1 Feb. 1818, pp. 73.

---

NOTES

⚙ Skill: Media

How ideas remain relevant from one medium to another can be illustrated by a modern doctor quoting "Ozymandias" during surgery. In "A Strange Relativity: Altered Time for Surgeon-Turned Patient."

Dr. Paul Kalanithi expresses a desire to accomplish something in the time he has left.

This reminds me of how the once colossal accomplishment in "Ozymandias" is now a ruin.

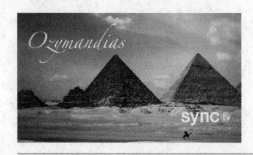

# First Read

Read "Ozymandias." After you read, complete the Think Questions below.

## ☁ THINK QUESTIONS

1. How does the traveler in the poem describe the statue and the area that surrounds it? Cite specific details from the text to support your response.

2. In the inscription on the pedestal, what does the term *works* refer to? Use specific details from the text to support your answer.

3. In the video "A Strange Relativity: Altered Time for Surgeon-Turned-Patient," Paul Kalanithi explains that "clocks are now kind of irrelevant to me." Do you think the speaker of "Ozymandias" would agree with this opinion about time? Use evidence from the poem to support your response.

4. Use context to determine the meaning of the word **pedestal** as it is used in line 9 of the poem "Ozymandias." Write your definition of *pedestal* here, and tell how you determined its meaning. Then write a synonym for this term. Check your inferred meaning of *pedestal* in a dictionary. Consult a print or digital dictionary or a thesaurus to verify the synonym you wrote.

5. Use context to determine the meaning of the word **colossal** as it is used in line 13 of the poem "Ozymandias." Check the etymology and part of speech of the word in a general or specialized dictionary or in another reference. Then write the definition of *colossal* here, and explain how it is derived from the Greek.

# Skill:
# Media

Use the Checklist to analyze Media in "Ozymandias." Refer to the sample student annotations about Media in the text.

To identify multiple interpretations of a story, drama, or poem, do the following:

✓ Note the similarities and differences in different media, such as the live production of a play or a recorded novel or poetry.

✓ Evaluate how each version interprets the source text.

✓ Consider how, within the same medium, a story can have multiple interpretations if told by writers from different time periods and cultures.

✓ Consider how stories told in the same medium will likely reflect the specific objectives as well as the respective ideas, concerns, and values of each writer.

To analyze multiple interpretations of a story, drama, or poem, evaluating how each version interprets the source text, consider the following questions:

✓ What medium is being used, and how does it affect the interpretation of the source text?

✓ What are the main similarities and differences between the two (or more) versions?

✓ If each version is from a different time period and/or culture, what does each version reveal about the author's objectives and the time period and culture in which it was written?

Please note that excerpts and passages in the StudySync® library and this workbook are intended as touchstones to generate interest in an author's work. The excerpts and passages do not substitute for the reading of entire texts, and StudySync® strongly recommends that students seek out and purchase the whole literary or informational work in order to experience it as the author intended. Links to online resellers are available in our digital library. In addition, complete works may be ordered through an authorized reseller by filling out and returning to StudySync® the order form enclosed in this workbook.

Reading & Writing
Companion

115

# Skill: Media

Reread lines 9–14 of "Ozymandias" and watch the StudySyncTV episode. Then use the Checklist on the previous page to answer the multiple-choice questions below.

## ⟳ YOUR TURN

1. In the clip, Dr. Kalanithi describes his relationship with time. How do his words reflect the theme shown in these lines of "Ozymandias"?

   ○ A. Even a doctor, someone in a position of power, or on a "pedestal," can be struck down by illness, much like the rulers of ancient Egypt.

   ○ B. Medical training, like the "king of kings," wants to show power over the future, but time extends beyond all of us.

   ○ C. Cancer, like the decay mentioned in the poem, causes "despair" and a "colossal wreck" for all of its victims.

   ○ D. Being a surgeon, like "the colossal wreck," often results in financial and personal stress, causing pain over time.

2. What is the **most likely** reason the video included scenes from Dr. Kalanithi and his family enjoying a Thanksgiving meal?

   ○ A. The video is a tribute to Dr. Kalanithi's family and friends and the memories they share.

   ○ B. The video was made to remind Dr. Kalanithi's family and friends to live each day to the fullest.

   ○ C. The video evokes the idea of gratitude for the time we have on Earth, even if that time is short.

   ○ D. The video uses the scenes to underscore the theme of the importance of family.

# Close Read

Reread "Ozymandias." As you reread, complete the Skills Focus questions below. Then use your answers and annotations from the questions to help you complete the Write activity.

## ◎ SKILLS FOCUS

1. Identify a detail that contributes to an overall theme in the poem, and write a sentence that explains why you chose it.

2. All sonnets contain a *volta*, which means "turn" in Italian. More specifically, a *volta* is a turning point in which there is a shift in language, style, meaning, or tone. Highlight the *volta* in "Ozymandias," and explain how it represents a turning point.

3. The words on the pedestal of Ozymandias' statue are "My name is Ozymandias, king of kings: / Look on my works, ye Mighty, and despair!" How does the video of Dr. Kalanithi influence or change your reading of these words?

4. Most of this sonnet repeats the story told by "a traveller." What is the power of this story "from an antique land?" Why is the narrator of the poem repeating what he heard the traveller say?

## ✏ WRITE

LITERARY ANALYSIS: The scholar and literary critic Donald H. Reiman has stated that Shelley "dedicated his efforts to the destruction of tyranny in all its forms." In the video "A Strange Relativity," Dr. Paul Kalanithi invokes "Ozymandias" while reflecting on his new relationship with time, which he describes as "peculiar and free." Write a short essay indicating whether you find evidence of a philosophy of destroying the tyranny of time in "Ozymandias." How accurate is the interpretation put forth in the video? Remember to use textual evidence to support your claim.

# Frankenstein

FICTION
Mary Shelley
1818

## Introduction

Mary Shelley (1797–1851) began writing *Frankenstein* as a teenager as part of a competition among her friends to write the best horror story. First published in 1818, this gothic tale of scientific experimentation gone wrong is now considered one of the earliest examples of science fiction. The novel's main character, Dr. Frankenstein, has discovered a way to reanimate dead tissue using an electrical current. His experiment is a success, but the result is a monster brought to life. Horrified by the creature he has created, the doctor flees. Alone and confused, the monster accidentally kills Dr. Frankenstein's younger brother and then murders his best friend. In the excerpts here, both the doctor and the monster come to terms with their intertwined fates.

# "I was benevolent and good; misery made me a fiend."

from Chapter 5

1   It was on a dreary night of November that I beheld the accomplishment of my toils. With an anxiety that almost amounted to agony, I collected the instruments of life around me, that I might **infuse** a spark of being into the lifeless thing that lay at my feet. It was already one in the morning; the rain pattered dismally against the panes, and my candle was nearly burnt out, when, by the glimmer of the half-extinguished light, I saw the dull yellow eye of the creature open; it breathed hard, and a convulsive motion agitated its limbs.

2   How can I describe my emotions at this catastrophe, or how delineate the wretch whom with such infinite pains and care I had endeavoured to form? His limbs were in proportion, and I had selected his features as beautiful. Beautiful! Great God! His yellow skin scarcely covered the work of muscles and arteries beneath; his hair was of a lustrous black, and flowing; his teeth of a pearly whiteness; but these luxuriances only formed a more horrid contrast with his watery eyes, that seemed almost of the same colour as the dun-white sockets in which they were set, his shrivelled complexion and straight black lips.

3   The different accidents of life are not so changeable as the feelings of human nature. I had worked hard for nearly two years, for the sole purpose of infusing life into an inanimate body. For this I had deprived myself of rest and health. I had desired it with an ardour that far exceeded moderation; but now that I had finished, the beauty of the dream vanished, and breathless horror and disgust filled my heart. Unable to endure the aspect of the being I had created, I rushed out of the room and continued a long time traversing my bed-chamber, unable to compose my mind to sleep. At length **lassitude** succeeded to the tumult I had before endured, and I threw myself on the bed in my clothes, endeavouring to seek a few moments of forgetfulness. But it was in vain; I slept, indeed, but I was disturbed by the wildest dreams. I thought I saw Elizabeth,[1] in the bloom of health, walking in the streets of Ingolstadt. Delighted and surprised, I embraced her, but as I imprinted the first kiss on her lips, they became livid with the hue of death; her features appeared to change, and

1. **Elizabeth** the fiancée of Victor Frankenstein

I thought that I held the corpse of my dead mother in my arms; a shroud enveloped her form, and I saw the grave-worms crawling in the folds of the flannel. I started from my sleep with horror; a cold dew covered my forehead, my teeth chattered, and every limb became convulsed; when, by the dim and yellow light of the moon, as it forced its way through the window shutters, I beheld the wretch—the miserable monster whom I had created. He held up the curtain of the bed; and his eyes, if eyes they may be called, were fixed on me. His jaws opened, and he muttered some inarticulate sounds, while a grin wrinkled his cheeks. He might have spoken, but I did not hear; one hand was stretched out, seemingly to detain me, but I escaped and rushed downstairs. I took refuge in the courtyard belonging to the house which I inhabited, where I remained during the rest of the night, walking up and down in the greatest **agitation,** listening attentively, catching and fearing each sound as if it were to announce the approach of the demoniacal corpse to which I had so miserably given life.

. . .

from Chapter 10

4   As I said this, I suddenly beheld the figure of a man, at some distance, advancing towards me with superhuman speed. He bounded over the crevices in the ice, among which I had walked with caution; his stature, also, as he approached, seemed to exceed that of man. I was troubled; a mist came over my eyes, and I felt a faintness seize me, but I was quickly restored by the cold gale of the mountains. I perceived, as the shape came nearer (sight tremendous and abhorred!) that it was the wretch whom I had created. I trembled with rage and horror, resolving to wait his approach and then close with him in mortal combat. He approached; his countenance bespoke bitter anguish, combined with disdain and malignity, while its unearthly ugliness **rendered** it almost too horrible for human eyes. But I scarcely observed this; rage and hatred had at first deprived me of utterance, and I recovered only to overwhelm him with words expressive of furious detestation and contempt.

5   "Devil," I exclaimed, "do you dare approach me? And do not you fear the fierce vengeance of my arm wreaked on your miserable head? Begone, vile insect! Or rather, stay, that I may trample you to dust! And, oh! That I could, with the extinction of your miserable existence, restore those victims whom you have so diabolically murdered!"

6   "I expected this reception," said the daemon. "All men hate the wretched; how, then, must I be hated, who am miserable beyond all living things! Yet you, my creator, detest and spurn me, thy creature, to whom thou art bound by ties only dissoluble by the annihilation of one of us. You purpose to kill me. How dare you sport thus with life? Do your duty towards me, and I will do mine towards you and the rest of mankind. If you will comply with my

Copyright © BookheadEd Learning, LLC

NOTES

conditions, I will leave them and you at peace; but if you refuse, I will glut the maw of death, until it be satiated with the blood of your remaining friends."

7 "Abhorred monster! Fiend that thou art! The tortures of hell are too mild a vengeance for thy crimes. Wretched devil! You reproach me with your creation, come on, then, that I may extinguish the spark which I so negligently bestowed."

8 My rage was without bounds; I sprang on him, impelled by all the feelings which can arm one being against the existence of another.

9 He easily eluded me, and said, —

10 "Be calm! I entreat you to hear me before you give vent to your hatred on my devoted head. Have I not suffered enough, that you seek to increase my misery? Life, although it may only be an accumulation of anguish, is dear to me, and I will defend it. Remember, thou hast made me more powerful than thyself; my height is superior to thine, my joints more supple. But I will not be tempted to set myself in opposition to thee. I am thy creature, and I will be even mild and docile to my natural lord and king if thou wilt also perform thy part, which thou owest me. Oh, Frankenstein, be not equitable to every other and trample upon me alone, to whom thy justice, and even thy **clemency** and affection, is most due. Remember that I am thy creature; I ought to be thy Adam, but I am rather the fallen angel, whom thou drivest from joy for no misdeed. Everywhere I see bliss, from which I alone am irrevocably excluded. I was benevolent and good; misery made me a fiend. Make me happy, and I shall again be virtuous."

---

## ✏ WRITE

PERSONAL RESPONSE: Dr. Frankenstein reflects on his creation, "For this I had deprived myself of rest and health. I had desired it with an ardour that far exceeded moderation; but now that I had finished, the beauty of the dream vanished, and breathless horror and disgust filled my heart." Write an essay in which you reflect on a time you invested a substantial amount of time and energy to create, earn, or obtain something you believed was important but then had an unexpected reaction to the finished product. What lessons did you learn, and how does this connect to Frankenstein's reaction? Include relevant evidence from the text to support your response.

Please note that excerpts and passages in the StudySync® library and this workbook are intended as touchstones to generate interest in an author's work. The excerpts and passages do not substitute for the reading of entire texts, and StudySync® strongly recommends that students seek out and purchase the whole literary or informational work in order to experience it as the author intended. Links to online resellers are available in our digital library. In addition, complete works may be ordered through an authorized reseller by filling out and returning to StudySync® the order form enclosed in this workbook.

Reading & Writing Companion    121

Extended Writing Project and Grammar

EXTENDED WRITING PROJECT
RESEARCH WRITING

# Research Writing Process: Plan

| PLAN | DRAFT | REVISE | EDIT AND PUBLISH |
|------|-------|--------|------------------|

As the Industrial Revolution transformed Britain in the eighteenth and nineteenth centuries, the English Romantic poets sought inspiration in the beauty of the natural world. Romanticism's passionate defense of and nostalgia for nature have continued to this day, represented in environmental movements.

## WRITING PROMPT

### How can we better value nature through our daily behaviors?

Think of a daily behavior that the average person may not know is damaging to nature. For example, people may not think about reducing their use of plastic bags when cleaning up after their dogs or may not consider the consequences of constantly upgrading their phones and other technology. Research your topic, and structure your essay to be clear, informative, and convincing. Then write a research essay, using both informative text structures and source materials to support your claim and make your informative essay convincing. Be sure to include the following elements:

- an introduction that clearly expresses your thesis on a topic related to daily behaviors and their impact on nature
- a clear thesis statement that informs and engages the reader
- a clear and logical informative text structure
- a formal style with an appropriate register and purposeful vocabulary, tone, and voice
- a conclusion that wraps up your ideas
- a works cited page

### Writing to Sources

As you gather ideas and information from the texts in the unit, be sure to:

- use evidence from multiple sources.
- avoid overly relying on one source.

Please note that excerpts and passages in the StudySync® library and this workbook are intended as touchstones to generate interest in an author's work. The excerpts and passages do not substitute for the reading of entire texts, and StudySync® strongly recommends that students seek out and purchase the whole literary or informational work in order to experience it as the author intended. Links to online resellers are available in our digital library. In addition, complete works may be ordered through an authorized reseller by filling out and returning to StudySync® the order form enclosed in this workbook.

Reading & Writing Companion    123

## Introduction to Research Writing

Research writing examines a researchable topic and presents information supported by evidence from a variety of reliable sources. The characteristics of research writing include:

- a clear thesis statement that presents a claim about your topic

- supporting details from a variety of sources

- a text structure that organizes ideas in a clear, impactful, and convincing manner

- a conclusion that rephrases the thesis

- in-text citations and a works cited page

As you continue with this Extended Writing Project, you'll receive more instruction and practice in crafting each of the characteristics of research writing to create your own research paper.

Before you get started, read this research essay that one student, Rishal, wrote in response to the writing prompt. As you read the Model, highlight and annotate the features of informative research writing that Rishal included in his essay.

## ☰ STUDENT MODEL

### Nurture Nature

#### A Damaging Relationship

1    Did you know that it takes on average sixty-six days to establish a habit? Yet, in today's fast-paced world, many people do not stop and think about how their daily habits impact the environment around them. Although nature isn't always a consideration when going through our daily routine, even the smallest decisions and behaviors can have a lasting impact on the environment, either positively or negatively. Humans did not always have such a damaging relationship with the environment. The great civilizations of the past, such as ancient Greece, celebrated nature instead of trying to dominate it. Things started to change during the Industrial Revolution. Nonetheless, during the 1800s, Romantic writers praised nature and were skeptical of industrial development. Two-hundred years later, the environment is rarely something we think about while going through our daily lives. With more and more damage being done to the environment, we need to take action to reduce the harmful daily burdens we place on the environment due to our behaviors, habits, and choices.

#### An Unexpected Truth

2    One of the daily behaviors that is unexpectedly damaging to the environment is recycling. This common, well-meaning habit isn't as good for the environment as people tend to think. When people think about how to reduce the amount of trash in their community, they usually think mainly of recycling.

NOTES

## 28% OF AMERICANS LIVE IN AREAS SEEN TO **STRONGLY ENCOURAGE** RECYCLING

% OF US ADULTS WHO SAY PEOPLE IN THEIR LOCAL COMMUNITY _____ RECYCLING AND RE-USE.

| STRONGLY ENCOURAGE | ENCOURAGE BUT ARE NOT OVERLY CONCERNED | DO NOT ENCOURAGE |
|---|---|---|
| 28% | 48% | 22% |

NOTE: RESPONDENTS WHO DID NOT GIVE AN ANSWER ARE NOT SHOWN. SOURCE: SURVEY CONDUCTED MAY 10-JUNE 6 2016 PEW RESEARCH CENTER

"The Politics of Climate." Pew Research Center, Washington, D.C. October 4, 2016. http://www.pewresearch.org/fact-tank/2016/10-07/perceptions-and-realities-of-recycling-vary-widely-from-place-to-place/

As this graph demonstrates, almost 80 percent of U.S. communities encourage recycling, according to data collected by the Pew Research Center. Many cities and towns have recycling containers in public places, and some even provide them individually to homes and office buildings. Recently, however, recycling has become a less helpful option for improving the environment.

### A New Challenge

3   Americans recycle nearly seventy million tons of material per year (Albeck-Ripka). Previously, most of this material went to China for processing. This was because China is the largest processor of recycled materials in the world. All that changed in 2018. China announced that it would temporarily stop accepting recycled material from other countries. The Chinese produced enough recyclable material within its own borders to meet its needs. It threatened to make the changes permanent.

4   What this means is that the United States suddenly had to figure out what to do with tons and tons of materials collected for recycling. There are too few factories in our country to process such a large quantity of recyclables. Other nations such as Indonesia and Vietnam have such factories, but they can handle only a fraction of the amount that China used to process. The Los Angeles Times Editorial Board said of the situation in California: "Bales of mixed paper (cereal boxes, junk mail and the like) and plastics are piling up in warehouses up and down the state." Some communities have even started depositing their recyclables in landfills.

**An Inefficient Process**

5   As the following NBC News footage of a recycling plant shows, recycling even a fraction of these seventy million tons is not a clean and easy process. In these ten seconds of video, we hear considerable sound pollution, see piles of waste being moved around by machinery, and clouds of exhaust pouring out of a factory in Seattle, Washington. This short glimpse into the process gives us a sense of how wasteful even recycling can be.

**A Simple Solution**

6   Yet, what are we to do with our trash if recycling is no longer the best answer?

7   The answer is simple: We must produce less trash.

8   Where do we start?

9   When looking where to start trash reduction programs, we need look no further than plastic. Many people do not even bother recycling plastics and other trash and just throw them in the garbage. The garbage is taken to landfills. While landfills may seem like a viable solution, some parts of the United States are running out of space for landfills. For example, the Northeast has to pay neighboring states to accept its trash because the region no longer has adequate space to manage its own landfills ("Roundup of Successful Waste Reduction Campaigns by Cities").

10  Plastic trash takes the longest to biodegrade, or break down. For example, a plastic shopping bag takes at least ten years to break down. A plastic soft drink bottle takes about 450 years to biodegrade (New Hampshire Department of Environmental Services). When people don't throw plastic waste into a recycle bin or even a garbage can, nature can be seriously harmed. For instance, fish mistake the plastic for food and die after eating it. Huge sections of the Pacific Ocean are covered with plastic trash that has drifted out to sea and been collected together by currents. This, in combination with climate change, has created huge "dead zones" where there is little life near the ocean's surface. All of the marine life near the surface suffers from a lack of oxygen. The plastic also blocks out sunlight, interfering with photosynthesis in tiny plants called phytoplankton. These plants form the base of the oceanic food chain.

11   Another problem with plastic is that it does not recycle well. Most plastics can be recycled into lower-quality material that is only useful for cheap products like synthetic fabric and bumper stickers (Somerville). In addition, factories that recycle plastics require a great deal of energy, often generating greenhouse gases and other pollution. Although we should continue to recycle as much paper as we have factory space for, recycling plastic is much less efficient.

**A Growing Community**

12   Some people have already started working on the problem. As the graph below shows, approximately 75 percent of U.S. adults are concerned for the environment, and 20 percent consistently take action as a result of that concern. This is a community that must keep growing, and effective strategies for trash reduction are already emerging.

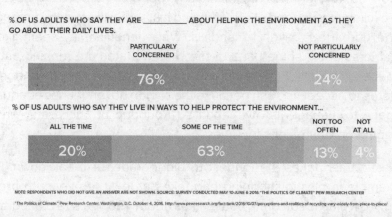

**MOST AMERICANS REPORT CONCERN FOR THE ENVIRONMENT; ONE-IN-FIVE TRY TO ACT ON THAT CONCERN ALL THE TIME**

% OF US ADULTS WHO SAY THEY ARE _____ ABOUT HELPING THE ENVIRONMENT AS THEY GO ABOUT THEIR DAILY LIVES.

| PARTICULARLY CONCERNED | NOT PARTICULARLY CONCERNED |
|---|---|
| 76% | 24% |

% OF US ADULTS WHO SAY THEY LIVE IN WAYS TO HELP PROTECT THE ENVIRONMENT...

| ALL THE TIME | SOME OF THE TIME | NOT TOO OFTEN | NOT AT ALL |
|---|---|---|---|
| 20% | 63% | 13% | 4% |

NOTE: RESPONDENTS WHO DID NOT GIVE AN ANSWER ARE NOT SHOWN. SOURCE: SURVEY CONDUCTED MAY 10-JUNE 6 2016 "THE POLITICS OF CLIMATE" PEW RESEARCH CENTER

"The Politics of Climate." Pew Research Center, Washington, D.C. October 4, 2016. http://www.pewresearch.org/fact-tank/2016/10/07/perceptions-and-realities-of-recycling-vary-widely-from-place-to-place/

13   One of the most effective strategies is banning stores from giving out plastic shopping bags. In Kenya, a ban on plastic bags has resulted in cleaner waterways and a less contaminated food supply chain (Watts). After the state of California banned plastic shopping bags, there was a drop in the amount of litter on beaches. Manufacturers of plastic shopping bags have lobbied heavily against these laws. Another campaign against plastic involves plastic straws. Seattle has banned plastic straws and plastic utensils in restaurants. "Plastic pollution is surpassing crisis levels in the world's oceans, and

I'm proud Seattle is leading the way and setting an example for the nation by enacting a plastic straw ban," Seattle Public Utilities General Manager Mami Hara said (CBS News). The city was inspired by a similar ban in Great Britain. India has announced it will institute the same type of ban in several years. Each community that takes action against plastic waste inspires other communities to do the same.

**A Huge Difference**

14  We can make a huge difference if we all change our daily routines. Individuals can take easy and immediate action and make better decisions when it comes to their impact on nature, especially when it comes to recycling. For example, when you order carry-out, ask that no plastic utensils or straws be included.

15  Staying informed will help you adjust your daily routines to respond to new facts and discoveries in the field. By sharing your research and the strategies you've implemented, you can support your friends and family members in understanding the problem and help them value nature in a more sustainable, beneficial manner.

16  Nature needs to be nurtured. Nature provides us with food, water, and the air we breathe. Yet, in return, some of our choices and behaviors damage it. Nature should be a source of inspiration. We need to be advocates for nature, just as the Romantic writers were. William Wordsworth said it best: "Come forth into the light of things; let nature be your teacher."

### Works Cited

Albeck-Ripka, Livia. "Your Recycling Gets Recycled, Right? Maybe, or Maybe Not." *The New York Times,* 29 May 2018, www.nytimes. com/2018/05/29/climate/ Recycling-landfills-plastic-papers.html. Accessed 20 Oct. 2018.

Anderson, Monica. "For Earth Day, Here's How Americans View Environmental Issues." *Pew Research Center,* 20 Apr. 2017, http:// www.pewresearch.org/fact-tank/2017/04/20/for-earth-day-heres-how-americans-view-environmental-issues/. Accessed 31 Dec. 2018.

CBS News. "Seattle Becomes First U.S. City to Ban Plastic Utensils and Straws." *CBS News*, 2 Jul. 2018, www.cbsnews.com/news/seattle-becomes-first-u-s-city-to-ban-plastic-utensils-and-straws/. Accessed 20 Oct. 2018.

Dean, Signe. "Here's How Long It Really Takes to Break a Habit, According to Science." *Science Alert,* 9 Jun. 2018, www.sciencealert.com/how-long-it-takes-to-break-a-habit-according-to-science. Accessed 21 Nov. 2018.

Desilver, Drew. "Perceptions and Realities of Recycling Vary Widely From Place to Place." *Pew Research Center*, 7 Oct. 2016, http://www.pewresearch.org/fact-tank/2016/10/07/perceptions-and-realities-of-recycling-vary-widely-from-place-to-place/ft16-10-05recyclingencouraged/. Accessed 31 Dec. 2018.

Lakeshore Recycling Services. "Roundup of Successful Waste Reduction Campaigns by Cities." *Lakeshore Recycling Services*, 25 Apr. 2018. www.lrsrecycles.com/ roundup-successful-waste-reduction-campaigns-cities/. Accessed 31 Dec. 2018.

Los Angeles Times Editorial Board. "California Has a Recycling Crisis." *The Los Angeles Times,* 26 May 2018, www.latimes.com/opinion/editorials/la-ed-recycling-crisis-20180526-story.html. Accessed 20 Oct. 2018.

NBC News X Press. "Recycling Center." *NBC News X Press*, 25 Jun. 2018. https://www.nbcnewsarchivesxpress.com/contentdetails/1937321. Accessed 23 Nov. 2018.

New Hampshire Department of Environmental Services. "Approximate Time It Takes Garbage to Decompose in Its Environment." New Hampshire Department of Environmental Services, 23 Mar. 2017, www.des.nh.gov/organization/ divisions/water/wmb/coastal/trash/documents/marinedebris.pdf. Accessed 7 Jan. 2019.

Scientific American. "'Dead' Sea of Plastic Bottles." *Scientific American*, www.scientificamerican.com/article/dead-sea-of-plastic-bottles/. Accessed 2 Oct. 2018.

Somerville, Madeleine. "Yes, You Recycle. But Until You Start Reducing, You're Still Killing the Planet." *The Guardian,* 19 May 2016, www.theguardian.com/lifeandstyle/ 2016/jan/19/eco-friendly-living-sustainability-recycling-reducing-saving-the-planet. Accessed 20 Oct. 2018.

Watts, Jonathan. "Eight Months On, Is the World's Most Drastic Plastic Bag Ban Working?" *The Guardian,* 25 Apr. 2018, https://www.theguardian.com/world/2018/apr/25/nairobi-clean-up-highs-lows-kenyas-plastic-bag-ban. Accessed 20 Oct. 2018.

Please note that excerpts and passages in the StudySync® library and this workbook are intended as touchstones to generate interest in an author's work. The excerpts and passages do not substitute for the reading of entire texts, and StudySync® strongly recommends that students seek out and purchase the whole literary or informational work in order to experience it as the author intended. Links to online resellers are available in our digital library. In addition, complete works may be ordered through an authorized reseller by filling out and returning to StudySync® the order form enclosed in this workbook.

Reading & Writing Companion

131

**WRITE**

When writing, it is important to consider your audience and purpose so you can write appropriately for them. Reread the prompt to determine your purpose for writing.

To begin, review the questions below, and then select a strategy, such as brainstorming, journaling, reading, or discussing, to generate ideas.

- **Topic:** What topic about the human impact on nature do you find most interesting?
- **Purpose:** What is your reason for writing? What message do you want to express?
- **Audience:** Who is your audience? How will knowing your audience help you write a better essay?
- **Questions:** What do you want to learn about your topic? What questions do you want to research?

**Response Instructions**

Use the questions in the bulleted list to write a one-paragraph research summary. Your summary should include possible research questions based on the prompt.

This is your first step in writing a research essay. As you progress through this Extended Writing Project, you will develop a research plan and will have opportunities to critique your research plan at each step of the writing process. If necessary, you will be able to implement changes. For example, as you begin reviewing sources, you may find that your major research question is too broad. If so, you can modify your major research question and then refocus and revise your research plan as needed.

# Skill:
# Planning Research

To conduct a short or more sustained research project to answer a question or solve a problem, do the following:

- Select a topic or problem to research.

- Think about what you want to find out and what kind of research can contribute to the project.

- Start to formulate your major research question by asking open-ended questions that begin "How. . .?" and "Why. . .?" and then choose a question you are interested in exploring.

- Synthesize multiple sources on the subject to look at information from different points of view, while demonstrating understanding of the subject under investigation.

To conduct a short or more sustained research project to answer a question or solve a problem, consider the following questions:

- Does my major research question allow me to explore a new issue, an important problem worth solving, or a fresh perspective on a topic?

- Can I research my question within my given time frame and with the resources available to me?

- Have I synthesized multiple sources on the question or problem, looking for different points of view?

- Have I demonstrated understanding of the subject under investigation in my research project?

Please note that excerpts and passages in the StudySync® library and this workbook are intended as touchstones to generate interest in an author's work. The excerpts and passages do not substitute for the reading of entire texts, and StudySync® strongly recommends that students seek out and purchase the whole literary or informational work in order to experience it as the author intended. Links to online resellers are available in our digital library. In addition, complete works may be ordered through an authorized reseller by filling out and returning to StudySync® the order form enclosed in this workbook.

Reading & Writing
Companion

**133**

## ↻ YOUR TURN

Read the research questions below. Then complete the chart by sorting the questions into the correct category. Write the corresponding letter for each question in the appropriate column.

| | Research Questions |
|---|---|
| A | Why do people choose to spend time outdoors? |
| B | Why did the bald eagle become an endangered species? |
| C | How does pollution lead to microplastics in the ocean or carcinogens in the air? |
| D | What are major pollutants in the world today? |
| E | How has America treated wild animals throughout its history? |
| F | How does pollution affect air and water quality in the U.S.? |
| G | Does hiking make people live longer? |
| H | How are endangered species currently being protected in the U.S.? What can be improved? |
| I | How does spending time outdoors or in nature affect people's health and mood? |

| Topic | Too Narrow | Appropriate | Too Broad |
|---|---|---|---|
| Endangered Species | | | |
| Pollution | | | |
| Spending Time Outdoors | | | |

## ⟳ YOUR TURN

Develop a research question for formal research. Then write a short plan for how you will go about doing research for your essay.

| Process | Plan |
|---|---|
| Research Question | |
| Step 1 | |
| Step 2 | |
| Step 3 | |
| Step 4 | |

Please note that excerpts and passages in the StudySync® library and this workbook are intended as touchstones to generate interest in an author's work. The excerpts and passages do not substitute for the reading of entire texts, and StudySync® strongly recommends that students seek out and purchase the whole literary or informational work in order to experience it as the author intended. Links to online resellers are available in our digital library. In addition, complete works may be ordered through an authorized reseller by filling out and returning to StudySync® the order form enclosed in this workbook.

Reading & Writing
Companion

135

# Skill:
# Evaluating Sources

## ••• CHECKLIST FOR EVALUATING SOURCES

Once you gather your sources, identify the following:

- where information seems inaccurate, biased, or outdated
- where information strongly relates to your task, purpose, and audience
- where information helps you make an informed decision or solve a problem

To conduct advanced searches to gather relevant, credible, and accurate print and digital sources, use the following questions as a guide:

- Are there specific terms or phrases I can use to adjust my search?
- Can I use *and*, *or*, or *not* to expand or limit my search?
- Can I use quotation marks to search for exact phrases?
- Is the material published by a well-established source or expert author?
- Is the material up to date or based on the most current information?
- Is the material factual, and can it be verified by another source?
- Are there discrepancies between the information presented in different sources?

**YOUR TURN**

Read the sentences below. Then complete the chart by sorting the sentences into two categories: those that are credible and reliable and those that are not. Write the corresponding letter for each sentence in the appropriate column.

| | Sentences |
|---|---|
| **A** | The article was published recently and uses up-to-date information. |
| **B** | The text uses only one viewpoint or relies on opinions instead of cited sources. |
| **C** | The text includes many viewpoints that are properly cited. |
| **D** | The article was published many years ago and uses statistics that may be outdated. |
| **E** | The article includes clear arguments and counterarguments that are supported by factual information. |
| **F** | The website is a personal blog or social media website. |

| Credible and Reliable | Not Credible or Reliable |
|---|---|
| | |
| | |
| | |

**YOUR TURN**

Complete the chart below by filling in the title and author of a source for your informative research essay and answering the questions about this source.

| Component and Questions | Answers |
|---|---|
| **Source Title and Author:** | |
| **Reliability:** Has the source material been published in a well-established book or periodical or on a well-established website? Is the source material up to date or based on the most current information? | |
| **Accuracy:** Is the source based on factual information that can be verified by another source? Are there any discrepancies between this source and others? | |
| **Credibility:** Is the source material written by a recognized expert on the topic? Is the source material published by a well-respected author or organization? | |
| **Decision:** Should I use this source in my research essay? | |

# Skill:
# Research and Notetaking

## ••• CHECKLIST FOR RESEARCH AND NOTETAKING

To conduct short as well as more sustained research projects to answer a question (including a self-generated question) or solve a problem, note the following:

- Answer a question for a research project, or think of your own question that you would like to have answered.

- Look up your topic in an encyclopedia to find general information.

- Find specific, up-to-date information in books and periodicals or on the Internet. If appropriate, conduct interviews with experts to get information.

- Narrow or broaden your inquiry when appropriate.

  > If you find dozens of books on a topic, your research topic may be too broad.

  > If it is difficult to write a research question, narrow your topic so it is more specific.

- Synthesize your information by organizing your notes from various sources to see what your sources have in common and how they differ.

To conduct short as well as more sustained research projects to answer a question (including a self-generated question) or solve a problem, consider the following questions:

- What is my research question?

- Where could I look to find information?

- How does new information I have found affect my research question?

- How can I demonstrate my understanding of the subject I am investigating?

YOUR TURN

Read each point from Rishal's note cards below. Then complete the chart by sorting the points into two categories: those that support reexamining our relationship with recycling and those that support reducing waste consumption. Write the corresponding letter for each point in the appropriate column.

| Points | |
|---|---|
| A | Source 5: Processing plastic for reuse provides low-quality material that can be used only for cheap products. |
| B | Source 3: A plastic soft drink bottle takes about 450 years to biodegrade, or break down. |
| C | Source 6: The Northeastern United States has run out of room for landfills. |
| D | Source 8: As NBC News footage of a recycling plant shows, recycling even a fraction of these seventy million tons is not a clean and easy process. |
| E | Source 4: The situation after China's ban on foreign garbage: "bales of mixed paper (cereal boxes, junk mail and the like) and plastics are piling up in warehouses up and down the state." |
| F | Source 7: "Plastic pollution is surpassing crisis levels in the world's oceans." |

| Reexamine Our Relationship with Recycling | Reduce Waste Consumption |
|---|---|
| | |
| | |
| | |

WRITE

Use the questions in the Checklist to locate sources and synthesize the information about one point or idea related to your topic in a paragraph for your draft.

# Research Writing Process: Draft

| PLAN | DRAFT | REVISE | EDIT AND PUBLISH |
|------|-------|--------|------------------|

You have already made progress toward writing your research essay. You have developed a research plan; selected a major research question; and located, evaluated, and synthesized information from a variety of sources. Before you begin drafting, you should take a moment to critique your research plan and implement any changes needed. For example, now that you have done your background reading and research, you may want to refine your thesis or claim or clarify the points you plan to make in your essay.

Now it is time to draft your research essay.

## WRITE

Use your plan and other responses in your Binder to draft your essay. You may also have new ideas as you begin drafting. Feel free to explore those new ideas as you have them. You can also ask yourself these questions to ensure that your writing is focused and organized and you have elaborated on your ideas:

**Draft Checklist:**

☐ **Purpose and Focus:** Have I made my claim clear to readers? Will they understand the purpose of my research? Have I included only relevant information and details and nothing extraneous that might confuse my readers?

☐ **Organization:** Does the organizational structure in my essay make sense? Will readers be engaged by the organization and interested in the way I present information and evidence?

☐ **Evidence and Elaboration:** Have I provided sufficient evidence and elaboration? Will my readers be able to follow my ideas and details?

Before you submit your draft, read it over carefully. You want to be sure that you've responded to all aspects of the prompt.

Please note that excerpts and passages in the StudySync® library and this workbook are intended as touchstones to generate interest in an author's work. The excerpts and passages do not substitute for the reading of entire texts, and StudySync® strongly recommends that students seek out and purchase the whole literary or informational work in order to experience it as the author intended. Links to online resellers are available in our digital library. In addition, complete works may be ordered through an authorized reseller by filling out and returning to StudySync® the order form enclosed in this workbook.

Reading & Writing Companion

141

Here is Rishal's research essay draft. As you read, notice how Rishal develops his draft to be focused and organized, so it has relevant evidence and elaboration to support his claim. As he continues to revise and edit his informative research essay, he will find and improve weak spots in his writing, as well as correct any language or punctuation mistakes.

Copyright © Bookheaded Learning, LLC

---

**NOTES**

## ≡ STUDENT MODEL: FIRST DRAFT

### Nurture Nature

~~Although nature isn't always a consideration when going through our daily routine, even the smallest decisions and behaviors can have a lasting impact on the environment, either positively or negatively. Modern society seems more focused on economic gain and "progress" at the expense of the environment. The great civilizations of the past, such as ancient Greece, celebrated nature instead of trying to dominate it. In the 1800s, Romantic writers praised nature and were sceptical of industrial development. With more and more damage being done to the environment, we need to take action to reduce the amount of trash that is dumped in the natural world.~~

A Damaging Relationship

Did you know that it takes on average sixty-six days to establish a habit? Yet, in today's fast-paced world, many people do not stop and think about how their daily habits impact the environment around them. Although nature isn't always a consideration when going through our daily routine, even the smallest decisions and behaviors can have a lasting impact on the environment, either positively or negatively. Humans did not always have such a damaging relationship with the environment. The great civilizations of the past, such as ancient Greece, celebrated nature instead of trying to dominate it. Things started to change during the Industrial Revolution. Nonetheless, during the 1800s, Romantic writers praised nature and were skeptical of industrial development. Two-hundred years later, the environment is rarely something we think about while going through our daily lives. With more and more damage being done to the environment, we need to take action to reduce the harmful daily burdens we place on the environment due to our behaviors, habits, and choices.

**Skill: Print and Graphic Features**

*Rishal adds a heading to signal to his readers what the paragraph will be about. As he rereads his draft, he will continue to add headings to help organize his information effectively.*

When people think about how to reduce the amount of trash in their community, they usually think first of recycling. Many cities and towns have recycling containers in public places, and some even provide them individually to homes and office buildings. Americans recycle nearly seventy million tons of material per year (Albeck-Ripka).

~~We must produce less trash. When looking where to start trash reduction programs, we need look no further than plastic. Fish mistake the plastic for food and die after eating it. Plastic trash takes practically forever to biodegrade. When people are too lazy to be responsible and throw plastic waste into a recycle bin or even a garbage can, defenseless creatures are forced to suffer! Huge sections of the Pacific Ocean are covered with plastic trash that has drifted out to sea and been collected together by currents. Gross! This, in combination with climate change, has created huge hypoxic areas where there is little life near the ocean's surface. The plastic also interferes with the photosynthesis of phytoplankton, which form the base of the oceanic trophic pyramid.~~

Plastic trash takes the longest to biodegrade, or break down. For example, a plastic shopping bag takes at least ten years to break down. A plastic soft drink bottle takes about 450 years to biodegrade (New Hampshire Department of Environmental Services). When people don't throw plastic waste into a recycle bin or even a garbage can, nature can be seriously harmed. For instance, fish mistake the plastic for food and die after eating it. Huge sections of the Pacific Ocean are covered with plastic trash that has drifted out to sea and been collected together by currents. This, in combination with climate change, has created huge "dead zones" where there is little life near the ocean's surface. All of the marine life near the surface suffers from a lack of oxygen. The plastic also blocks out sunlight, interfering with photosynthesis in tiny plants called phytoplankton. These plants form the base of the oceanic food chain.

Another problem with plastic is that it does not recycle well. Most plastics can be recycled into awful material that is only fairly awful and only good for cheap products like sinthetick fabric and bumper stickers (*The Guardian*). And, factories that recycle plastics require a great deal of energy, often with greenhouse gases and other

 **Skill: Critiquing Research**

As he revises, Rishal thinks about how to synthesize and integrate information from multiple sources. In this paragraph, he adds relevant information from the New Hampshire Department of Environmental Services.

pollution. Although we should continue to recycle as much paper as we have factory space for, recycling plastic is much less effishient.

For example, the Northeast has to pay nayboring states to accept its trash. It's run out of room for it ("Roundup of Successful Waste Reduction Campaigns by Cities"). Many people do not even bother recycling plastics and other trash and just throw them in the garbage. The garbage is taken to landfills. It's now at the point that some parts of the United States are running out of space for landfills.

~~All of this means that our top priority should be programs that reduce the amount of plastic waste and some people have already started work on the problem because one of the most effective strategies is banning stores from giving out plastic shopping bags. In Kenya, a ban on plastic bags has resulted in cleaner waterways and a less contaminated food supply chain. After the state of California banned plastic shopping bags, there was a drop in the amount of litter on beaches. Manufacturers of plastic shopping bags have lobbyed heavily against these laws. Another campaign against plastic involves plastic straws. Seattle has banned plastic straws and plastic utensils in restaurants. Plastic pollution is serpassing crisis levels in the world's oceans, and I'm proud Seattle is leading the way and setting an example for the nation by enacting a plastic straw ban, Seattle Public Utilities General Manager Mami Hara said. The city was inspired by a similar ban in Great Britain. India has announced it will institute the same type of ban in several years. Each community that takes action against plastic waste inspires other communities to do the same.~~

One of the most effective strategies is banning stores from giving out plastic shopping bags. In Kenya, a ban on plastic bags has resulted in cleaner waterways and a less contaminated food supply chain (Watts). After the state of California banned plastic shopping bags, there was a drop in the amount of litter on beaches. Manufacturers of plastic shopping bags have lobbied heavily against these laws. Another campaign against plastic involves plastic straws. Seattle has banned plastic straws and plastic utensils in restaurants. "Plastic pollution is surpassing crisis levels in the world's oceans, and I'm proud Seattle is leading the way and setting an example for the nation by enacting a plastic straw ban," Seattle Public Utilities

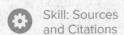

**Skill: Sources and Citations**

*Even though Rishal attributed the statement about Seattle's plastic straw ban to Mami Hara, he needs to cite the source of the remark, so he inserts a parenthetical citation. Since the source is electronic, he doesn't have to include a page number.*

General Manager Mami Hara said (CBS News). The city was inspired by a similar ban in Great Britain. India has announced it will institute the same type of ban in several years. Each community that takes action against plastic waste inspires other communities to do the same.

As individuals, we shouldn't rely on our local leaders do all the work on waste. We can make a huge difference if we all change our daily routines. Take a reusable bag to the store when you shop. If you forget to take a reusable bag to the store when you shop, ask for a paper bag. You can also make a difference when you order carry out. When you order carry out, ask that no plastic utensils or straws be included. Support businesses that use biodegradable containers instead of plastic. Tell your friends and family members about the problem, and share ways to fix it with them.

Nature needs to taken care of. Nature should be a source of inspiration. We need to be advocates for nature, just as the Romantic writers were. William Wordsworth said it best: "Come forth into the light of things; let nature be your teacher."

## Works Cited

Albeck-Ripka, Livia. "Your Recycling Gets Recycled, Right? Maybe, or Maybe Not," *The New York Times*, 29 May 2018, www.nytimes.com/2018/05/29/climate/ recycling-landfills-plastic-papers.html

"Approximate Time It Takes Garbage to Decompose in Its Environment." New Hampshire Department of Environmental Services. www.des.nh.gov/organization/divisions/water/wmb/coastal/trash/documents/marine_debris.pdf.

CBS News. "Seattle Becomes First U.S. City to Ban Plastic Utensils and Straws," 2 Jul. 2018. www.cbsnews.com/news/seattle-becomes-first-u-s-city-to-ban-plastic-utensils-and-straws

Lakeshore Recycling Services. "Roundup of Successful Waste Reduction Campaigns by Cities." Blog, 4/25/2018. www.lrsrecycles.com/ roundup-successful-waste-reduction-campaigns-cities/

Somerville, Madeleine. "Yes, You Recycle. But Until You Start Reducing, You're Still Killing the Planet." *The Guardian*, 19 May

Please note that excerpts and passages in the StudySync® library and this workbook are intended as touchstones to generate interest in an author's work. The excerpts and passages do not substitute for the reading of entire texts, and StudySync® strongly recommends that students seek out and purchase the whole literary or informational work in order to experience it as the author intended. Links to online resellers are available in our digital library. In addition, complete works may be ordered through an authorized reseller by filling out and returning to StudySync® the order form enclosed in this workbook.

Reading & Writing Companion    **145**

2016, www.theguardian.com/lifeandstyle/ 2016/jan/19/ eco-friendly-living-sustainability-recycling-reducing-saving-the-planet

Watts, Jonathan. "Eight Months On, Is the World's Most Drastic Plastic Bag Ban Working?" *The Guardian*, 4/25/2018, www.theguardian.com/world/2018/apr/25/nairobi-clean-up-highs-lows-kenyas-plastic-bag-ban.

**CRITIQUING RESEARCH**

Sync•skills

# Skill:
# Critiquing Research

To conduct short or sustained research projects to answer a question or solve a problem, drawing on several sources, do the following:

- Narrow or broaden the question or inquiry as necessary when researching your topic.

- Use advanced search terms effectively when looking for information online, such as using unique terms that are specific to your topic (i.e., "daily life in Jamestown, Virginia" rather than only "Jamestown, Virginia").

- Assess the strengths and limitations of each source in terms of the task, purpose, and audience.

- Synthesize and integrate information from multiple sources to maintain a flow of ideas and avoid overly relying on one single source.

- Quote or paraphrase the information you have found without plagiarizing, or copying, your source.

- Provide information about your sources in a bibliography or another standard format for citations.

To evaluate and use relevant information while conducting short or sustained research projects, consider the following questions:

- Did I narrow or broaden my research inquiry as needed?

- Have I successfully synthesized and integrated information from multiple sources on my topic to maintain a flow of ideas and avoid overly relying on one single source?

- Did I quote or paraphrase information without plagiarizing?

Please note that excerpts and passages in the StudySync® library and this workbook are intended as touchstones to generate interest in an author's work. The excerpts and passages do not substitute for the reading of entire texts, and StudySync® strongly recommends that students seek out and purchase the whole literary or informational work in order to experience it as the author intended. Links to online resellers are available in our digital library. In addition, complete works may be ordered through an authorized reseller by filling out and returning to StudySync® the order form enclosed in this workbook.

Reading & Writing Companion    147

## ⟳ YOUR TURN

Choose the best answer to each question.

1.  Below is the introduction from a student's draft, which explains why conservation is important. As he researches, the student discovers that restoration ecology may be more effective for saving endangered species. How should he replace his underlined thesis statement?

> Biodiversity is the variety of life in an environment. A healthy ecosystem needs to be biodiverse. When one species go extinct, other species often follow. Scientists had not realized that extinction occurs until late in the eighteenth century, so the concept was still relatively new to Romantics. Even so, they realized the threat extinction posed to nature, and so they began the conservation movement to protect rare plants and animals. <u>Conservation has been successful in rescuing many species, but it is important to maintain efforts to protect the environment.</u>

- ○ A. Conservation has been ineffective in preventing extinction in many cases.
- ○ B. Humans are the primary cause of extinction in the modern world.
- ○ C. Biodiversity is essential to our understanding of how environments work.
- ○ D. However, it is not enough to conserve; damaged ecosystems need to be restored.

2.  Rishal came across the following information and source in his research about recycling. What should he do?

> Recycled products contain the energies of previous products, and their previous uses will determine the characteristic of the new product that will be made from the recycled material.
>
> Source: www.conspiracy.blog.com

- ○ A. Modify his research question.
- ○ B. Consider if the source is appropriate.
- ○ C. Rewrite his thesis using the new information.
- ○ D. Revise his research plan.

## ✏ WRITE

Use the questions in the Checklist to critique your research process to determine whether you need to modify your major research question, revise your research plan, or change any other aspect of your research essay.

# Skill:
# Sources and Citations

To gather relevant information from multiple authoritative print and digital sources and to cite the sources correctly, do the following:

- Gather information from a variety of print and digital sources, using search terms effectively to narrow your search.

- Find information on authors to see whether they are experts on a topic.

- Avoid relying on any one source, and synthesize information from a variety of books, publications, and online resources.

- Quote or paraphrase the information you find, and cite it to avoid plagiarism.

- Integrate information selectively to maintain a logical flow of ideas in your essay, using transitional words and phrases.

- Include all sources in a bibliography, following a standard format:

  > Halall, Ahmed. *The Pyramids of Ancient Egypt*. New York: Central Publishing, 2016.

  > For a citation, footnote, or endnote, include the author, title, and page number.

To check that you have gathered information and cited sources correctly, consider the following questions:

- Did I cite the information I found using a standard format to avoid plagiarism?

- Did I include all my sources in my bibliography?

Please note that excerpts and passages in the StudySync® library and this workbook are intended as touchstones to generate interest in an author's work. The excerpts and passages do not substitute for the reading of entire texts, and StudySync® strongly recommends that students seek out and purchase the whole literary or informational work in order to experience it as the author intended. Links to online resellers are available in our digital library. In addition, complete works may be ordered through an authorized reseller by filling out and returning to StudySync® the order form enclosed in this workbook.

Reading & Writing Companion    **149**

**YOUR TURN**

Choose the best answer to each question.

1.  Below is a section from a previous draft of Rishal's research paper. Which change should Rishal make to improve the clarity of his citations?

> According to Megan Forbes on the National Oceanic and Atmospheric Administration (NOAA) Ocean Podcast episode "Garbage Patches: How Gyres Take Our Trash Out to Sea," there are at least three major patches of "concentrated (and mostly plastic) marine debris" in our oceans (Forbes).

- ○ A.  Add the page number after the author's name in the parentheses.
- ○ B.  Remove the citation in parentheses after the quotation.
- ○ C.  Remove the quotation marks around the cited material.
- ○ D.  No change needs to be made.

2.  Below is a section from a previous draft of Rishal's works cited page in the MLA format. Which revision best corrects his style errors?

> Thompson, *James. Landfill Waste Costs Continued to Rise in 2016. Solid Waste Environmental Excellence Protocol*, 12 Jan. 2017. https://nrra.net/sweep/cost-to-landfill-waste-continues-to-rise-through 2016/

- ○ A.  Thompson, James. "Landfill Waste Costs Continued to Rise in 2016." Solid Waste Environmental Excellence Protocol, 12 Jan 2017. https://nrra.net/sweep/cost-to-landfill-waste-continues-to-rise-through-2016/
- ○ B.  *Landfill Waste Costs Continued to Rise in 2016*. by James Thompson. *Solid Waste Environmental Excellence Protocol*, 12 Jan 2017. https://nrra.net/sweep/cost-to-landfill-waste-continues-to-rise-through-2016/
- ○ C.  "Landfill Waste Costs Continued to Rise in 2016." by James Thompson. *Solid Waste Environmental Excellence Protocol*, 12 Jan. 2017. https://nrra.net/sweep/cost-to-landfill-waste-continues-to-rise-through-2016/
- ○ D.  Thompson, James. "Landfill Waste Costs Continued to Rise in 2016." *Solid Waste Environmental Excellence Protocol*, 12 Jan. 2017, https://nrra.net/sweep/cost-to-landfill-waste-continues-to-rise-through-2016/. Accessed 31 Dec. 2018.

 **WRITE**

Use the questions in the Checklist to create or revise your in-text citations and works cited list.

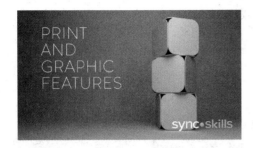

# Skill:
# Print and Graphic Features

## ••• CHECKLIST FOR PRINT AND GRAPHIC FEATURES

First, reread your draft, and ask yourself the following questions:

- To what extent would including formatting, graphics, or multimedia be effective in achieving my purpose?
- Which formatting, graphics, or multimedia seem most important in conveying information to the reader?
- How is the addition of the formatting, graphics, or multimedia useful in aiding comprehension?

To include formatting, graphics, and multimedia, use the following questions as a guide:

- How can I use formatting to better organize information? Consider adding:
  - > titles
  - > headings
  - > subheadings
  - > bullets
  - > boldface and italicized terms

- How can I use graphics to better convey information? Consider adding:
  - > charts
  - > graphs
  - > tables
  - > timelines
  - > diagrams
  - > figures and statistics

- How can I use multimedia to add interest and variety? Consider adding a combination of:
  - > photographs
  - > art
  - > audio
  - > video

**YOUR TURN**

Choose the best answer to each question.

1. Reread the paragraph from Rishal's draft. Which of the following headings best represents the content of the passage and would help his audience focus on the main idea?

> We must produce less trash. When looking where to start trash reduction programs, we need look no further than plastic. Fish mistake the plastic for food and die after eating it. Plastic trash takes practically forever to biodegrade. When people are too lazy to be responsible and throw plastic waste into a recycle bin or even a garbage can, defenseless creatures are forced to suffer! Huge sections of the Pacific Ocean are covered with plastic trash that has drifted out to sea and been collected together by currents. Gross! This, in combination with climate change, has created huge hypoxic areas where there is little life near the ocean's surface. The plastic also interferes with the photosynthesis of phytoplankton, which form the base of the oceanic trophic pyramid.

- ○ A. Stop the Plastics Lobby Today
- ○ B. The Most Harmful Everyday Material
- ○ C. Oceans Are Not Landfills
- ○ D. Climate Change and Recycling

2. Rishal also considers adding an image, graph, or table to help his audience understand how extensive plastic waste is. Which of the following graphic elements would be most helpful to readers?

- ○ A. An image of a water bottle floating in the ocean with wildlife nearby
- ○ B. A table depicting the increase in recycling facilities worldwide
- ○ C. A graphic displaying the effect of climate change on the world's oceans
- ○ D. An image showing large quantities of plastic waste in the ocean

 **WRITE**

Use the questions in the Checklist to add at least three headings, two graphics, and one piece of multimedia to your research essay.

RESEARCH
WRITING
PROCESS
REVISE

# Research Writing Process: Revise

| PLAN | DRAFT | REVISE | EDIT AND PUBLISH |
|------|-------|--------|------------------|

You have written a draft of your research essay. You have also received input from your peers about how to improve it. Now you are going to revise your draft.

## ◄◄ REVISION GUIDE

Examine your draft to find areas for revision. Keep in mind your purpose and audience as you revise for clarity, development, organization, and style. Use the guide below to help you review.

| Review | Revise | Example |
|--------|--------|---------|
| **Clarity** | | |
| Reread the concluding paragraph of your research essay. | Make sure you rephrase your thesis or claim in a new way to remind readers of the purpose of your research and topic. | Nature needs to ~~taken care of~~ be nurtured. Nature provides us with food, water, and the air we breathe. Yet, in return, some of our choices and behaviors damage it. Nature should be a source of inspiration. We need to be advocates for nature, just as the Romantic writers were. William Wordsworth said it best: "Come forth into the light of things; let nature be your teacher." |

| Review | Revise | Example |
|--------|--------|---------|
| **Development** | | |
| Highlight a key detail used to support your claim. | Strengthen your essay by supporting key details with evidence from reputable sources. Make sure to include any additional sources in your works cited list. | Plastic trash takes ~~practically forever~~ the longest to biodegrade, or break down. For example, a plastic shopping bag takes at least ten years to break down. A plastic soft drink bottle takes about 450 years to biodegrade (New Hampshire Department of Environmental Services). When people ~~are too lazy to be responsible and~~ don't throw plastic waste into a recycle bin or even a garbage can, ~~defenseless creatures are forced to suffer!~~ nature can be seriously harmed. |
| **Organization** | | |
| Review your body paragraphs. Are they organized? Does information flow from one paragraph to the next? Identify and annotate any sentences within and across paragraphs that don't flow in a clear and logical way. | Rewrite the sentences so they appear in a clear and logical order. | For example, the Northeast has to pay nayboring states to accept its trash. ~~It's run out of room for it~~ because the region no longer has adequate space to manage its own landfills (Lakeshore Recycling Services). ~~Many people do not even bother recycling plastics and other trash and just throw them in the garbage. The garbage is taken to landfills. It's now at the point that some parts of the United States are running out of space for landfills.~~ |

Copyright © BookheadEd Learning, LLC

| Review | Revise | Example |
|---|---|---|
| **Style: Word Choice** | | |
| Identify any weak adjectives or verbs. | Replace weak adjectives and verbs with strong, descriptive adjectives and verbs. | ~~Tell your friends and family members about the problem, and share ways to fix it with them.~~ By sharing your research and the strategies you've implemented, you can support your friends and family members in understanding the problem and help them value nature in a more sustainable, beneficial manner. |
| **Style: Sentence Fluency** | | |
| Read aloud your writing, and listen to the way the text sounds. Does it sound choppy? Or does it flow smoothly with rhythm, movement, and emphasis on important details and events? | Rewrite a key passage, making your sentences longer or shorter to achieve a better flow of writing. Remove repetitive phrases. | We can make a huge difference if we all change our daily routines. ~~Take a reusable bag to the store when you shop. If you forget to take a reusable bag to the store when you shop, ask for a paper bag. You can also make a difference when you order carry out. When you order carry out, ask that no plastic utensils or straws be included.~~ Individuals can take easy and immediate action and make better decisions when it comes to their impact on nature, especially when it comes to recycling. For example, when you order carryout, ask that no plastic utensils or straws be included. |

### ✏ WRITE

Use the Revision Guide, as well as your peer reviews, to help you evaluate your research essay to determine places you should revise both within and between sentences.

# Skill:
# Using a Style Guide

To make sure your writing conforms to the guidelines in a style manual, do the following:

- Determine which style guide you should use before you write your draft.

  > Follow the guidelines chosen by a teacher, for example.

  > Familiarize yourself with that guide, and check your writing against the guide when you edit.

- Use the style guide for the overall formatting of your paper, citation style, bibliography format, and other style considerations for reporting research.

- As you draft, use an additional style guide, such as *Artful Sentences: Syntax as Style* by Virginia Tufte, to help you vary your syntax, or the grammatical structure of sentences.

  > Use a variety of simple, compound, complex, and compound-complex sentences to convey information.

  > Be sure to punctuate your sentences correctly.

  > Follow standard English language conventions to help you maintain a formal style for formal papers.

To edit your work so that it conforms to the guidelines in a style manual, consider the following questions:

- Have I followed the conventions for spelling, punctuation, capitalization, sentence structure, and formatting according to the style guide?

- Have I varied my syntax to make my information clear for readers?

- Do I have an entry in my works cited or bibliography for each reference I used?

- Have I followed the correct style, including the guidelines for capitalization and punctuation, in each entry in my works cited or bibliography?

**YOUR TURN**

Read the types of information below. Then complete the chart by sorting them into two categories: those that are found in a style guide and those that are not. Write the corresponding letter for each type of information in the appropriate column.

| Types of Information | | | |
|---|---|---|---|
| **A** | a list of possible research topics | **F** | the definition of a word |
| **B** | how to select a thesis | **G** | when to use italics |
| **C** | how to cite internet sources | **H** | synonyms for a word |
| **D** | how to write an outline | **I** | when to use a hyphen |
| **E** | how to format a bibliography | **J** | proper punctuation for quotations |

| In a Style Guide | Not in a Style Guide |
|---|---|
|  |  |
|  |  |
|  |  |
|  |  |
|  |  |

**✏ WRITE**

Use the Checklist to help you choose a convention that you have found challenging to follow. Use a credible style guide to check and correct any errors related to that convention in your research essay.

# Grammar: Contested Usage

For most formal writing, it is probably advisable to follow the traditional rules of grammar. In most cases, following the rules will improve both the clarity and effectiveness of your communication. However, there are a number of grammar "rules" that can be broken if you do it deliberately to improve the effectiveness of your writing.

| Contested Rules | Text |
|---|---|
| • Never begin a sentence with *And* or *But*.<br><br>• A paragraph must always consist of more than one sentence. | And now Miss Emily had gone to join the representatives of those august names where they lay in the cedar-bemused cemetery among the ranked and anonymous graves of Union and Confederate soldiers who fell at the battle of Jefferson.<br><br>A Rose for Emily |

People, and even references, often disagree about word usage. For one thing, new words enter the language all the time. An example of a current debate regarding usage involves the word *literally*. This word is sometimes used to emphasize a statement or description that is not literally true or possible. Some sources argue against this usage, explaining that it is illogical to use the word *literally* to mean "figuratively." And yet, even Mark Twain uses the word *literally* to describe things that could not be literally true. For instance:

| Text | Contested Usage |
|---|---|
| And when the middle of the afternoon came, from being a poor poverty-stricken boy in the morning, Tom was literally rolling in wealth.<br><br>The Adventures of Tom Sawyer | The character Tom Sawyer was not literally tumbling around in piles of money. |

If you are unsure whether it is acceptable to break a rule or if you want to resolve questions you may have about usage, you can always check a reference work on the subject. Several worth consulting are Merriam-Webster's *Dictionary of English Usage*, Bryan A. Garner's *Garner's Modern American Usage*, and Theodore Bernstein's *Miss Thistlebottom's Hobgoblins*. The Merriam-Webster Dictionary online also includes a Usage Guide for words that have been the subject of contested usage. For instance, if you look up the word *affect*, you will find a Usage Guide on the different uses of the word *affect* versus *effect*.

**YOUR TURN**

Choose the best answer to each question.

1. Which rule of usage has been deliberately broken in the text below?

   > Dost thou love life? Then do not squander time, for that is the stuff life is made of.
   > —Benjamin Franklin

   ○ A. Never begin a sentence with *Then*.

   ○ B. Never end a sentence with a preposition.

2. What evidence or source justifies the use of the word *ginormous* in the sentence below?

   > Can you really eat that <u>ginormous</u> sandwich?

   ○ A. The dictionary includes the word *ginormous* and recommends it for informal and humorous contexts.

   ○ B. Most grammar resources tell users to avoid using slang in formal writing.

3. Is the following sentence an example of how to break the rules of grammar in an effective way?

   > Knowledge of a particular time in history will help you better understand what an essay written during that time period is about.

   ○ A. Yes, the sentence ends with a preposition, which makes the last part of the sentence "what an essay written during that time period is about" clear and easy to read.

   ○ B. No, it would be clearer and more effective to follow the rules of grammar and change the last part of the sentence to "the content of an essay written during that time period."

4. Read the dialogue below. Which rule of grammar does this excerpt violate?

   > What is it, Papa?
   >
   > It's a treat. For you.
   >
   > What is it?
   >
   > Here. Sit down.
   >
   > from *The Road*, by Cormac McCarthy

   ○ A. Every line of dialogue needs to identify the speaker.

   ○ B. Dialogue needs to be set off by quotation marks.

DASHES
AND
HYPHENS

HYPHENS

sync•skills

# Grammar: Hyphens

Hyphens are mostly used to combine words, but they can also be used to divide words.

| Rule | Text |
|---|---|
| You may use a hyphen in a compound adjective that precedes a noun. | That **yearned-for** golden age became even more golden in the imaginations of later medieval writers, who enhanced Geoffrey's legend.<br><br>Unsolved Mysteries of History |
| Usually, hyphens are not needed to join a prefix to a word, but there are a few exceptions.<br><br>• Use a hyphen after any prefix joined to a proper noun or a proper adjective.<br><br>• Use a hyphen after the prefixes *all-*, *ex-* (meaning "former"), and *self-*.<br><br>• Generally, hyphens are used to avoid confusion, such as in words beginning with *re-* that could be mistaken for another word.<br><br>• Use a hyphen to separate the prefix *anti-* when it joins a word beginning with *i-*. | No complete parallel for the Cadbury fortification has been found anywhere else in **post-Roman** Britain.<br><br>Conversation with Geoffrey Ashe |
| Hyphens can be used to create compound nouns by joining words and giving them a unified meaning. | She had once been a lowly **maid-of-all-work** just like Amelia.<br><br>After the Ball |
| Hyphenate any compound word that is a spelled-out cardinal number (such as *twenty-one*) or ordinal number (such as *twenty-first*) up to *ninety-nine* or *ninety-ninth*. Hyphenate any spelled-out fraction. | She was **forty-six** years old, of average height and bearing, with an unremarkable face.<br><br>American Jezebel |

### ↻ YOUR TURN

Choose the best answer to each question.

1. How should this sentence be changed?

   > The world's population is growing at an alarming rate—fast enough to double in only forty-three years!

   ○ A. The world's population is—growing at an alarming rate—fast enough to double in only forty-three years!

   ○ B. The world's population is growing at an alarming rate—fast enough to double in only forty three years!

   ○ C. The world's population is growing at an alarming rate-fast enough to double in only forty-three years!

   ○ D. No change needs to be made to this sentence.

2. How should this sentence be changed?

   > The op-ed article—the one printed in the local paper—suggested that anti intellectual attitudes were threatening democracy.

   ○ A. The op—ed article—the one printed in the local paper—suggested that anti intellectual attitudes were threatening democracy.

   ○ B. The op-ed article-the one printed in the local paper-suggested that anti intellectual attitudes were threatening democracy.

   ○ C. The op-ed article—the one printed in the local paper—suggested that anti-intellectual attitudes were threatening democracy.

   ○ D. No change needs to be made to this sentence.

3. How should this sentence be changed?

   > John F. Kennedy was president of the United States from 1961 to 1963.

   ○ A. John F. Kennedy was president of the United States from 1961-to-1963.

   ○ B. John F. Kennedy was president of the United-States from 1961 to 1963.

   ○ C. John-F.-Kennedy was president of the United States from 1961 to 1963.

   ○ D. No change needs to be made to this sentence.

Please note that excerpts and passages in the StudySync® library and this workbook are intended as touchstones to generate interest in an author's work. The excerpts and passages do not substitute for the reading of entire texts, and StudySync® strongly recommends that students seek out and purchase the whole literary or informational work in order to experience it as the author intended. Links to online resellers are available in our digital library. In addition, complete works may be ordered through an authorized reseller by filling out and returning to StudySync® the order form enclosed in this workbook.

Reading & Writing Companion    **161**

# Research Writing Process: Edit and Publish

| PLAN | DRAFT | REVISE | EDIT AND PUBLISH |
|------|-------|--------|------------------|

You have revised your research essay based on your peer feedback and your own examination.

Now it is time to edit your research essay. When you revised, you focused on the content of your essay. You probably critiqued your research and made sure you paraphrased sources correctly and avoided plagiarism. When you edit, you focus on the mechanics of your essay, paying close attention to things like grammar and punctuation.

## Use the checklist below to guide you as you edit:

☐ Have I followed all the rules for hyphens?

☐ Can I defend any contested usage I have chosen? (Consult a style guide, such as *Artful Sentences: Syntax as Style* by Virginia Tufte, as appropriate.)

☐ Do I have any sentence fragments or run-on sentences?

☐ Have I spelled everything correctly?

## Notice some edits Rishal has made:

- Hyphenated a compound adjective preceding a noun

- Corrected spelling errors

- Corrected a citation to match the MLA style

- Started a sentence with a conjunctive adverb instead of the conjunction *and*

Another problem with plastic is that it does not recycle well. Most plastics can be recycled into ~~awful~~ lower-quality material that is only useful for cheap products like ~~sinthetick~~ synthetic fabric and bumper stickers (*~~The Guardian~~* Somerville). ~~And~~ In addition, factories that recycle plastics require a great deal of energy, often generating greenhouse gases and other pollution. Although we should continue to recycle as much paper as we have factory space for, recycling plastic is much less ~~effishient~~ efficient.

## ✏ WRITE

Use the questions in the Checklist, as well as your peer reviews, to help you evaluate your research essay to determine areas that need editing. Then edit your research essay to correct those errors.

Once you have made all your corrections, you are ready to publish your work. You can distribute your writing to family and friends, hang it on a bulletin board, or post it on your blog. If you publish online, share the link with your family, friends, and classmates.

Please note that excerpts and passages in the StudySync® library and this workbook are intended as touchstones to generate interest in an author's work. The excerpts and passages do not substitute for the reading of entire texts, and StudySync® strongly recommends that students seek out and purchase the whole literary or informational work in order to experience it as the author intended. Links to online resellers are available in our digital library. In addition, complete works may be ordered through an authorized reseller by filling out and returning to StudySync® the order form enclosed in this workbook.

Reading & Writing Companion **163**

PHOTO/IMAGE CREDITS:

cover, iStock.com/RMAX
p. iii, iStock.com/DNY59
p. ix, iStock.com/RMAX
p. x, Samuel Taylor Coleridge - Public Domain
p. x, John Keats - Leemage/Contributor/Hulton Fine Art Collection/Getty Images
p. x, D.H. Lawrence - Elliott & Fry/Contributor/Getty
p. x, John Locke - Public Domain
p. x, Mary Shelley - Heritage Images/Contributor
p. xi, Percy Bysshe Shelley - Art Collection 2/Alamy Stock Photo
p. xi, Jonathan Swift - iStock.com/GeorgiosArt
p. xi, Mary Wollstonecraft - Print Collector/Contributor/Getty
p. xi, William Wordsworth - Hulton Archive/Stringer/Hulton Archive/Getty Images
p. xii, ©iStock.com/Creativeye99
p. 1, Public Domain
p. 2, Getty: Universal History Archive/Contributor/Universal Images Group
p. 3, Getty: Photo Josse/Leemage/Contributor/Corbis Historical
p. 5, Culture Club/Hulton Archive/Getty Images
p. 7, ©iStock.com/Creativeye99
p. 8, iStock.com/wragg
p. 13, iStock.com/VvoeVale
p. 14, iStock/MarioGuti
p. 15, Hulton Deutsch/Corbis Historical/Getty Images
p. 16, picture alliance/picture alliance/Getty Images
p. 19, iStock.com/VvoeVale
p. 20, iStock.com/SarapulSar38
p. 29, ©iStock.com/Roberto A Sanchez
p. 30, Public domain
p. 36, ©iStock.com/Roberto A Sanchez
p. 37, ©iStock.com/yipengge
p. 38, ©iStock.com/yipengge
p. 39, ©iStock.com/Hohenhaus
p. 40, ©iStock.com/Hohenhaus
p. 41, ©iStock.com/janrysavy
p. 42, ©iStock.com/janrysavy
p. 43, ©iStock.com/Roberto A Sanchez
p. 44, iStock.com/leminuit
p. 51, iStock.com/leminuit
p. 52, iStock.com/ThomasVogel
p. 53, iStock.com/ThomasVogel
p. 54, iStock.com/pixhook
p. 55, iStock.com/pixhook
p. 56, iStock.com/leminuit
p. 57, iStock.com/vvvita
p. 59, Public Domain Image

p. 60, Public Domain Image
p. 62, iStock.com/vvvita
p. 63, iStock.com/Spectral-Design
p. 82, iStock.com/karelpesorna
p. 86, iStock.com/Alphotographic
p. 89, iStock.com/chuyu
p. 90, Print Collector/Hulton Fine Art Collection/Getty Images
p. 94, iStock.com/chuyu
p. 95, iStock.com/donatas1205
p. 96, iStock.com/donatas1205
p. 97, iStock.com/fotogaby
p. 98, iStock.com/fotogaby
p. 100, iStock.com/chuyu
p. 101, iStock.com/kutaytanir
p. 105, iStock.com/DaveBolton
p. 106, iStock/arogant
p. 108, iStock.com/DaveBolton
p. 109, iStock.com/Andrey_A
p. 110, iStock.com/Andrey_A
p. 111, iStock.com/DaveBolton
p. 112, iStock.com/
p. 113, DEA/S. VANNINI/De Agostini/Getty Images
p. 114, iStock.com/
p. 115, iStock.com/Hohenhaus
p. 116, iStock.com/Hohenhaus
p. 117, iStock.com/
p. 118, iStock.com/dwleindecker
p. 122, iStock.com/hanibaram, iStock.com/seb_ra, iStock.com/Martin Barraud
p. 123, iStock.com/Martin Barraud
p. 126, StudySync Graphic
p. 128, StudySync Graphic
p. 133, iStock.com/koya79
p. 136, iStock.com/Mutlu Kurtbas
p. 139, iStock.com/DNY59
p. 141, iStock.com/Martin Barraud
p. 147, iStock.com/SKrow
p. 149, iStock.com/tofumax
p. 151, iStock.com/me4o
p. 153, iStock.com/Martin Barraud
p. 156, iStock.com/Customdesigner
p. 158, ©iStock.com/wingmar
p. 160, ©iStock.com/Thomas Shanahan
p. 162, iStock.com/Martin Barraud

# studysync

## Text Fulfillment Through StudySync

If you are interested in specific titles, please fill out the form below and we will check availability through our partners.

## ORDER DETAILS

Date:

| TITLE | AUTHOR | Paperback/ Hardcover | Specific Edition *If Applicable* | Quantity |
|---|---|---|---|---|
|  |  |  |  |  |
|  |  |  |  |  |
|  |  |  |  |  |
|  |  |  |  |  |
|  |  |  |  |  |
|  |  |  |  |  |
|  |  |  |  |  |

### SHIPPING INFORMATION

Contact:

Title:

School/District:

Address Line 1:

Address Line 2:

Zip or Postal Code:

Phone:

Mobile:

Email:

### BILLING INFORMATION ☐ SAME AS SHIPPING

Contact:

Title:

School/District:

Address Line 1:

Address Line 2:

Zip or Postal Code:

Phone:

Mobile:

Email:

### PAYMENT INFORMATION

☐ CREDIT CARD

Name on Card:

Card Number:

Expiration Date:

Security Code:

☐ PO

Purchase Order Number:

StudySync Text Fulfillment, BookheadEd Learning, LLC
610 Daniel Young Drive | Sonoma, CA 95476